It's
Not Him,
It's
YOU

It's Not Him, It's YOU

THE TRUTH YOU MAY NOT WANT *BUT* *NEED* TO HEAR

Christie Hartman, PhD

Avon, Massachusetts

Published by
Adams Media, a division of F+W Media, Inc.
57 Littlefield Street, Avon, MA 02322. U.S.A.
www.adamsmedia.com

ISBN 10: 1-4405-0162-9
ISBN 13: 978-1-4405-0162-3

Printed in the United States of America.

10 9 8 7 6 5 4 3 2 1

Library of Congress Cataloging-in-Publication Data
is available from the publisher.

This publication is designed to provide accurate and authoritative
information with regard to the subject matter covered. It is sold with
the understanding that the publisher is not engaged in rendering
legal, accounting, or other professional advice. If legal advice or other
expert assistance is required, the services of a competent professional
person should be sought.

—From a *Declaration of Principles* jointly adopted
by a Committee of the American Bar Association
and a Committee of Publishers and Associations

Many of the designations used by manufacturers and sellers to distinguish their product are claimed as trademarks. Where those designations appear in this book and Adams Media was aware of a trademark
claim, the designations have been printed with initial capital letters.

This book is available at quantity discounts for bulk purchases.
For information, please call 1-800-289-0963.

This book is dedicated to all the single men and women who gave me the fodder to write this book. You know who you are! Your stories, anecdotes, opinions, complaints, advice, difficulties, and triumphs helped make this book what it is. Thank you, and may you find the right person for you.

Acknowledgments

A big, big thanks to my Handsome, who encouraged me and who stood by me during the stressful times. You're the best.

Contents

Introduction

Let's face it: sometimes dating sucks. Recently, I Googled the phrase "I hate dating" and got over 12,000 hits! The truth is, dating will challenge even the most confident woman. Dating forces us to face our imperfections, fears, and deepest insecurities. Yet, dating is necessary. Ask any single adult, male or female, why they bother with the difficulties of dating, and they'll all say the same thing: they're looking for the right person. If you want to meet Mr. Right, you have to get out there.

Of all the different phases of a relationship—from meeting to marriage—the earliest phase is definitely the most intimidating. Some of the challenges you face during this early phase include:

1. **Getting into the right mindset.** Do you have the right attitude? High standards? Without them, you won't meet Mr. Right.
2. **Meeting new men.** Where do you find the men? And how do you meet them? Checking out a cute guy is one thing, but breaking the ice with him is quite another.
3. **Going on those first few dates.** Does he seem interested? Is he a jerk? What if he doesn't call? The answers to these questions make or break most relationships.

This early phase, with the challenges it presents, is the most crucial to finding the right guy. *It is also when you're most likely to make mistakes.* If you don't identify these mistakes and correct them, you'll wind up frustrated, alone, or, worst of all, with the wrong guy.

It doesn't help matters that useful dating books are hard to find. Most so-called dating books are actually *relationship* books—they gloss over dating and focus on sex, the L word, or getting a guy to marry you. But without good dating skills, you won't find a guy worth having a relationship with, much less marrying! And some dating books focus more on making you laugh or telling you what you already know. While it's always good to laugh at yourself and to review the basics, sometimes you need more. I'll devote this entire book to the early dating challenges with the thorough attention they deserve! You'll learn that you, as a woman:

- Have the advantage over men in the dating world
- Should make the first move with men—not wait for them to act
- Can detect if a guy is truly interested in you, even before you go out with him

When it comes to dating, I've done the legwork. As a psychologist and researcher, I've done my share of dating research. I've talked to women and heard their dating frustrations. I've read the books, including ones written for men. I've read articles, perused advice columns, chatted in Internet forums, and researched dating services and online dating sites. I've also consulted the source: men. I've interviewed men and read dating advice on men's websites. I've hung out with countless men in social settings, including years of participation in outdoor sports, most of which are male-dominated. I've had countless male friends. And, finally, I've been out there in the trenches too, dating. What's my point here? This book is research-based, and everything you're going to learn has been thoroughly investigated.

In all of this research, I've found when women get frustrated with dating, the real problem isn't dating, or men. The problem is that during the early stages of dating, women unknowingly make one or more fundamental mistakes that hinder their ability to date successfully and find the man of their dreams. This book will identify each of these Top 10 mistakes, and show you how to fix them.

If you're reading this book, you're looking for something. Maybe you're looking for a relationship with a great guy. Perhaps you're even ready to get married and start a family and want to find the right guy to do that with. Or, maybe you just want to meet some men, go out on a few dates, and have some fun. No matter what you're looking for, it all starts with dating and dealing with men. And if you're reading this book, you've probably chosen the wrong guys in the past, been hit on by the wrong guys (and never the right ones!), put your best foot forward with a guy you really liked just to have him pull the rug out from under you, or had some other experiences that made you say, "Dating sucks." Whatever it is, if you aren't getting what you want out of dating, you'll find what you need here.

Dating isn't easy. But neither is starting a business, moving to a new city, or training for a marathon. These endeavors all have their stressful and difficult moments for sure, but isn't it worth it when your business takes off, you meet new friends, or you cross that finish line? Likewise, the hardships of dating are totally worth it when you meet the right guy. Dating success, like success in any area of life, comes from identifying your weak spots and working to improve them. Success is about *learning from your mistakes.* It's about knowing what you want, and not giving up until you find it. Anyone can tell you to wear a skirt or to avoid sex on the first date. But here you'll learn much more—how to understand and conquer the complexities of dating and find the man you want. Enjoy!

Mistake # 1

You Think Men Have a Clue

"Women know what men want.
Men know what men want.
What do we want?
We want women. That's it."

JERRY SEINFELD

If you read dating advice for men, written by men, male experts will often say that when it comes to dealing with women, there are two types of men: 1) Naturals, and 2) Everyone Else. Naturals have an almost inborn ease with women; they know how to talk to them, seem to understand them, and feel comfortable around them. It's not too surprising that Naturals have better luck with women—women gravitate toward Naturals without even realizing it. Why wouldn't we? Given a choice between the guy who compliments our new outfit and asks us about our career, versus the guy who stares at our boobs and blathers on about *his* career, the choice is obvious.

However, Naturals only comprise about 10 percent of men, at best. The other 90 percent have to learn the hard way how to attract women. Some learn quickly, some slowly, and some not at all. That is the first edict of this book: If you want to succeed in dating, you have to realize that when it comes to women, to some degree most men *do not have a clue.* This means that *you*, as a woman, have the advantage in dating.

Most men want a good woman in their lives, but they don't always know how to make that happen. Men will admit that they're clueless about women. Some will even say they could use a manual to help them understand women. Of course, there are many books on how to understand, attract, date, sleep with, and please women. But it's rare for a man to even search for a book about women or relationships, much less read one. They'll admit they don't understand women, but they won't ask for help because they won't admit that they can't figure out something for themselves. It's like the male stereotype about being lost: men will acknowledge they're lost, but then refuse to ask for directions!

I am not suggesting that men are dumb or inept. They aren't. While their cluelessness may frustrate you when you date them, it does give you a unique advantage. Although Mistake #1 is not the most obvious of the Top 10, it is the most fundamental to success in dating, which is why I list it first. Until you begin to see the advantage you have, you won't get the results you want.

How Can *I* Have the Advantage?

Up until now, you probably assumed men had a lot of the power in dating. After all, men usually do the asking out and the calling, right? And they can just as easily stop calling, right? Maybe you really liked a guy you went out with a few times and then you never heard from him again. Maybe you loved a guy who dragged his feet for three years about getting married. Or worse, maybe you had a guy sleep with you and then blow you off, or earn your trust and then cheat with another girl. When you've been through these sorts of things, you probably think it's insane to think that you have the advantage.

Many women assume that when men hurt us, it's because they have more power than we do, and can wield it in an uncaring way if they want to—much like our boss can make our job pleasurable or miserable. But in reality, when men hurt us, it's often because they don't understand us or don't know how to handle the pressures of dating. Sure, some men don't mind hurting women, but these men aren't the norm.

Having the advantage doesn't mean you'll never get rejected or hurt. It simply means that dating can be even harder for men than it is for women.

Why Men Don't Have the Upper Hand

When men disappoint or hurt us, it's easy to feel like they're selfish, cold-hearted creatures. However, it's important to realize that men find dating frustrating too. They want to find the right person too and they experience fear, disappointment, and hurt, just like we do.

When conducting research for this book, there is one thing that surprised me most: men think *we* have the power. Many men feel that women hold most of the cards in dating. And to some extent, they're right.

To illustrate this point, here are some examples of dating situations that make guys feel frustrated, hurt, and most of all, powerless:

- When women don't notice or pay attention to them
- When women don't find them attractive
- When women don't respond to their pickup attempts
- When women say no to being asked out
- When women don't return their phone calls or respond to e-mails
- When women want to "just be friends"
- When women pick some other guy over them
- When women don't want to have sex with them
- When women send mixed messages
- When women are rude or dismissive

Each one of the above situations makes men feel like women have all the power. Men envy the Naturals—the guys who have no problem attracting women and who always seem to have attractive women around. They also envy men who are rich, successful, or handsome because they know these things attract women. However, their envy will quickly disappear if these rich, successful, handsome guys, for whatever reason, have no women in their lives. If a guy can attract women, he's a success in the eyes of other men, even if he's coyote ugly or dirt poor.

Why am I telling you all of this? To show you how important women are to men. Sure, some men don't always want women for the right reasons or don't treat women right (you'll learn how to deal with these problems later in the book), but largely speaking, attracting women is of massive importance to men. That's the first piece of evidence to prove that you have a lot more power in dating than you think. You can't see the advantage you have when you date if you don't first recognize that men struggle with attracting women.

The next step is to show you *how* men struggle. Men not only struggle with dating as much as we do, in many ways they actually struggle more. The rest of this section will explain several reasons why.

Men Are Expected to Pursue

Everyone knows that, generally speaking, males are expected to pursue females, not the other way around. This isn't a hard-and-fast rule, and women will often initiate contact with men, but men, more than women, are still expected to do the calling, the asking out, and to generally make things happen. If they don't, they sit home alone eating fast food and playing video games. Call it biology, call it society's rules, but this is the way it is.

However, just because men are typically assigned the task of pursuing relationships with women does *not* mean that it's easy for them. On the contrary, it can be very difficult. While there's a certain power in being the pursuer, there is also a tremendous amount of *risk*. As the pursuers, men risk constant rejection and failure. Men *hate* rejection and failure.

I'm not saying women don't face rejection too; in fact, rejection is such a big deal that I devote all of Mistake #3 to this topic. But women can opt out of facing rejection up front by letting men approach them, letting men call them, letting men ask them out. Women can often get a date without much risk or trouble. Men don't have this luxury. If they don't face the dreaded possibility of rejection, they often remain dateless. This puts men at a disadvantage in dating.

Men Don't Understand Women

Many men don't understand women or know what women want. And they don't typically read dating or relationship books like women do. Many guys don't know how to approach women, how to talk to women, how to get them to go out, what they like in bed, or what will make them happy. Have you ever had some guy hit on you at a bar when you were just there to spend time with your girlfriends? Have you ever gone out with a guy who talked too much, interrupted you, or didn't ask you about yourself? Naturals know when and how to approach women, and they know that women want men who listen and take interest in what they have to say. Men can improve at these tasks with experience, but they have to work at it.

They say that if you want to make money selling a particular product, then you need to understand the buyer and her needs and concerns. Dating is no different—if a guy likes you, on some level he has to sell himself to you if he wants a chance. If he happens to have what you like, great. But if he doesn't understand women, he's more likely to get shut down.

Men Aren't As Good at Reading People

Part of getting people to like you comes from the ability to read people. Reading people is a fantastic skill in any area of life, but it's crucial in dating. Men can read people, but women are somewhat better at it. Women also tend to have better communication skills, leading to smoother and more comfortable interactions, which is important in dating. This relative lack of skill puts men at a disadvantage in dating because they don't always know how to read women's signs or how to communicate in the most effective way. For example, a guy is more likely to drone on about his job and not read his date's bored expression, or to put his hand on her leg and not see her discomfort, and then not understand why she doesn't call him back.

Men Don't Call the Shots

Men may pursue women, but women actually initiate most interactions with men through their body language. As you'll learn in Mistake #7, men don't usually pursue women until they get the green light. Women also initiate the majority of breakups and divorces; men are usually a couple of steps behind in understanding what went wrong, and why. Finally, women also decide whether sex is going to happen, and if so, when. For guys, the ability to call the sexual shots is a *huge* source of power that they feel is completely in women's hands. Overall, anyone who calls the shots, for whatever reason, has the advantage.

Men Aren't As Picky As Women

For many men, as long as a woman is physically attractive to him, she's a prospect, at least in the beginning. However, physical attractiveness isn't enough for many women, and women often have a whole repertoire of things beyond looks that they look for in men. As a result, men have to work harder to impress a woman up front than a woman does to impress a man. Again, this gives you the advantage.

If the above five reasons aren't enough evidence that men don't have the advantage in dating, get online. You will find more websites and articles devoted to how to attract women than those devoted to how to attract men. And check out the bookstore: there are a surprising number of books devoted to teaching men how to pick up women, get women to go out with them, get women to sleep with them, and to please women in bed. I've never seen a book that teaches a woman how to get a man into bed! By contrast, many men feel that all a woman needs to do to get a man is to be attractive and say the word. You may not agree with this, but if men believe it, that means you have the advantage. Overall, all these sources of information say the same thing: it's much easier for women to attract men than it is for men to attract women.

Men Know the Truth

Maybe you didn't know that women have the advantage over men in dating. But men know it. Most accept it and do the best they can to close the gap. But some men resent the power women have; they complain that women are capricious game-players who hold all the cards in dating, especially the sex card. Some men's advice encourages men to "take back" their power, to stop letting women walk all over them, and to start being "men" again. Some of this stuff is ridiculous, but if you look past the whining and mistrust of women, it comes down to the same problem: men want women, have little idea how to deal with them, and feel frustrated when they don't succeed.

When men don't succeed with women, they handle it in different ways. The wise ones try different things until they figure out what works, or they pick up a book on women and read it. But some men just stop trying and act passively, hoping a woman will land in their laps, or they get mad and resent women, as if women are to blame for their lack of success.

Moreover, a lot of dating advice for men revolves around trying to give men an advantage on what they feel is an uneven playing field. This is fine if the advice actually teaches men about women, which some of it does. But some of it also teaches men how to play games. Here are some things that men's dating gurus will tell them:

- Don't call her for at least five days after getting her number
- If you get too focused on one girl, take a bunch of other girls out (and sleep with them if you can)
- Don't tell her you love her unless she says it first
- Don't be too "nice" because women take advantage of nice guys
- Make fun of a woman to show her you aren't intimidated by her

No man would ever dispense (or follow) such advice unless he believed women had the advantage in dating. Feeling at a disadvantage is one reason why some men act like jerks to women.

Why Would We Think *Men* Call the Shots?

If you, like many women, have ever believed that men generally call the shots in dating, there's a good (and perhaps complicated) reason why. Here are some reasons why you might have developed this belief:

You've been hurt by men. As I mentioned earlier, if you've had bad experiences with men, it's easy to think they have the power because they were able to hurt you. For example, some women think men have a hard time being monogamous because they've dated men who cheated on them, refused to get married, or otherwise tried to conquer every woman in sight. If men were that hard to pin down, then they would have more power. But they aren't—most men want to and can make a commitment, *when they're ready to.* Anytime a guy disappoints, hurts, or rejects you, you will feel powerless to some extent. However, disappointment, hurt, and rejection are part of dating, and men experience them just as often.

You've made mistakes with men. Although mistakes are part of the drill in dating, perhaps you've made a few more mistakes than your friends. Maybe you're far too nice, letting men take advantage of you or take you for granted. Or perhaps you just have a knack for choosing bad guys. These mistakes will make you feel powerless with men, but this is due more to power you've given away rather than to any innate power that men have.

Other women and dating books say so. You don't have to look far to find a woman who thinks that men call the shots in dating, and some dating books operate on that basic idea. The more power they think men have, the more outrageous and gamey their advice will be.

Men have power in other areas. Because men hold positions of power in business and politics, you may unconsciously assume that they are the "powerful ones." Why wouldn't they call the shots in dating too? Historically (and even currently in some cultures), women weren't allowed to work or to own land, making them completely dependent on men—men did call the shots in those days. Times have certainly changed, but remnants of the old patriarchal tradition still exist.

Men get away with more. In the world of relationships, some men cheat, sleep around, or abandon children they didn't plan for. We're often told this is just "men being men." Who wouldn't look at such behavior and assume men must be pretty powerful to not only engage in such behavior without guilt, but to get away with it too? Women are judged more harshly.

Your family background taught you so. What you observed growing up will color your views on men and how they feel about women. If you grew up with a father who cared more about his work, his hobbies, or his mistress than he did about you or your mother, this sends you the message at a very young age that women aren't that important to men. Also, if you were raised in a very traditional home or in a culture that treats men like they're more important than women, you will often see men as powerful, even if you've rejected your family's traditions.

In general, any of the above may give you the impression that men are more powerful than they are. Men are powerful in many ways, but not when it comes to dating and women. They need women. Some men readily admit that finding a good woman is important to them, and they don't care who knows it. But other men don't like admitting this truth because they don't like admitting that they "need" anything. But get to know these men, and maybe get a few drinks in them, and they too will confess the truth.

Let the Games Begin . . .

If a woman feels that men call the shots in dating, she may contrive different kinds of games, ploys, or other behaviors in an attempt to gain the advantage. Here are some examples of this:

Playing Hard to Get

Playing hard to get is when a woman makes herself appear unobtainable or uninterested in the belief that men will find her more valuable or attractive. Here are a few examples of playing hard to get:

- Pretending you aren't interested in a guy because you think that men love a challenge

- Not looking at or talking to a guy who interests you because you're afraid you'll seem aggressive or turn him off
- Saying no to a date with a guy you're potentially interested in to see if he's serious about dating you and will try again
- Not calling a guy for a period of time so he'll wonder if something is wrong
- Not returning a man's calls and expecting him to call you again

Playing hard to get differs from being cautious or independent. Men do appreciate women who have lives of their own, and overly available women can appear desperate. But intentionally playing hard to get is unnecessary because, for most men, women *aren't* that easy to get. Men find approaching women and asking women out hard enough as it is, so if you feign disinterest, he'll usually give up. There are exceptions—some men like chasing women and want a challenge. But any guy who chases an uninterested woman and then gets bored because she decides she likes him has issues—and you're better off without him.

Being "Mysterious"

When it comes to dating, being mysterious means intentionally withholding information about yourself or making it difficult for a man to know where you stand. Being mysterious is similar to playing hard to get in that you're trying to keep a man at arm's length because you believe it will increase his interest and attraction to you. Early on, you shouldn't tell your life story, get too personal, or come on too strong—revealing yourself over time is always better.

But holding back too much only makes you look closed off and uncomfortable with yourself.

Heaping On the Sexuality

Women who want attention but don't understand what men find attractive will use the most powerful tool at their disposal: sex. You've seen these women; they dress in very revealing clothes and behave in overtly sexual ways. They think that's what it takes to get a man's attention. It works: you'll get their attention. But you'll only look like you're trying too hard or, worse, attract men who only want to sleep with you. Here's an example:

Ryan met a woman online and asked her to go to a baseball game. When she showed up at their meeting place, she was wearing very tight pants (with a hint of g-string showing), a skimpy top, really high heels, and lots of makeup. Ryan was turned off and did not call her again.

Remember: with sexiness, a little goes a long way.

Withholding Sex

Most women don't want to have sex with a guy until they know he's worth it. But some women see sex as a commodity you "give up" to a man rather than something you choose to share because you want to. These women believe sex, and the choice to share it, is the only power they have with men and so they covet it to get what they want. Not having sex until you're ready is powerful and an act of self-respect, but withholding sex because you're afraid a man won't respect you gives men a power they don't have.

Waiting for Men to Make the First Move

If you believe men will make the first move if they're truly interested, you think men have way more guts than they do. Most men will *not* make a move unless they think they have a good chance of success, which means they need some pretty obvious signs from you. If you sit back, hoping your good looks and cool disinterest will draw men to you, you won't get much action. Remember: men hate rejection too. This topic is so important that all of Mistake #7 is devoted to it.

Trying to Catch a Man

Some women treat finding a man like they're auditioning for a musical—they practically dance and sing to get a man to like them. They will chase men or go to great lengths to get noticed or asked out. For example, this type of woman might call a man all the time, pretend to be fascinated with hockey if it's his favorite sport, or spend all of her free time man-hunting. While it's often necessary to encourage a man and even to make the first move, you should never have to work to catch him—if he's interested, he'll come to you. If you work too hard to get a guy, you often wind up with the wrong guys.

What do all the above things have in common? They are all strategies designed to gain the upper hand with men, one way or another. But they backfire because they assume men have more power than they do. In many ways, women already have the upper hand! If you have to do any of the above things to get or keep a guy's interest, you're definitely dating the wrong kinds of guys in the wrong kinds of ways.

Power Dating

I've said that women have the advantage over men in dating. This means that in some ways, women have more *power* in the dating arena. The more you recognize the dating power you have, the more successful your dating life will be. But first you need to understand what this power is—and what it isn't.

Power is the ability to make things happen. However, we don't have much power over other people, including men. Some people manipulate or try to get others to do what they want, but this usually leads to frustration and a feeling of powerlessness. Ultimately, the only real power we have is over ourselves.

So how does this apply to dating? In dating, we control our actions and we choose how we handle things. We have little power over men and we can't make men do what we want. However, we can ask for what we want and, ultimately, choose to do what we want. Here are some examples:

You can't make a guy interested in you. However, you can dress nicely, talk to him, and show your interest, which will increase the odds of getting his interest. But if he doesn't seem interested or doesn't call you, you accept it and move on to someone else.

You can't make a guy treat you well. However, you can show him what you will or will not put up with, which will increase the odds that he'll shape up, or you can refuse to see him again and go pick a nicer guy.

You can't make a guy give you what you want. However, you can ask for what you want, increasing your odds of getting it, and you can choose to move on if he can't or won't give it to you.

Here are a few examples of a powerless versus powerful mindset.

Powerless Mindset	Powerful Mindset
You find a guy attractive and hope he'll come over and talk to you.	You smile or say hello, and see what he does.
You get mad at a guy because he's seeing other women, and pressure him to only see you.	You accept that he isn't ready for exclusivity, tell him that's what you're looking for, and move on.
You've had a string of bad dates and feel fed up with guys and dating.	You figure out what you could do to improve your dates and start doing it.

If you want to succeed in dating and find the right guy for you, not only do you have to recognize the power you have with men, but you should also recognize the power you have within yourself and how to use it. A powerful mindset makes for much better success in dating, whereas a powerless mindset only leaves you feeling frustrated.

Date Like a Powerful Woman

Now that you've learned the power you have as a woman and about the challenges men face in dating, here are some suggestions for a new way to approach dating. You'll learn more about all these points as you continue to read.

Use the powerful mindset. Whether looking for, meeting, or going out with men, your powerful mindset is your friend. No matter what the situation, remember that you always have a choice. For example, if a guy doesn't treat you right, you can choose to dump him or to explain to him how you want to be treated, knowing you can dump him if he doesn't get it right.

Remember that men are vulnerable too. As I've said, men hate and fear rejection just as much as women do. They want the same thing you do—to find someone who's right for them. The more you recognize this, the more you'll succeed with men.

Choose your men. You should be choosing the men who interest you, not waiting for men to choose you. Men know that approaching women is risky, so they won't always approach you if they're interested. If you wait to be chosen, you won't often get what you want.

Encourage men who interest you. Some eye contact, a smile, and a friendly hello will give a man the encouragement he needs to pursue something with you. Otherwise, the risk of rejection and embarrassment are too great for most men.

Focus on interested men. If you smile at or talk to a guy, or even go out with him a few times, make sure he's genuinely interested. When you waste time with men who aren't showing genuine interest, you throw away your advantage. Once a guy has shown a lack of interest, move on.

Avoid losers. Knowing that men want women and that there are tons of good guys who just need some encouragement from you, you don't need to waste time with jerks, players, bad boys, and other men who don't treat women right. You're at a huge disadvantage with these men. Many women who think men have all the power have spent too much time around losers.

Have compassion. Unless a guy is disrespectful, be kind to men who ask you out or show interest. Men have feelings too, even if they don't show them. If you aren't interested, be clear but be kind. Men may act confident, but it's hard for them to take that risk.

Despite everything you've learned in this section, it's important to remember that while you do have the advantage when you date, you don't have *all* the power. Men have power, too—they can stop calling you, reject you, or just refuse to do what you want them to. Having the advantage doesn't mean that everything will go your way, or that dating will be easy. It doesn't mean you won't get hurt or rejected. Having the advantage means that dating is often even more difficult for men than it is for women, and just knowing this will change how you approach dating and increase your success.

I hope that you now see how important women are to men, and how much say you have in your dating life. The rest of this book will expand upon this idea and show you how to use the power you have to make dating easier and more successful, and to get you the great guy you want.

Mistake #2

Your Attitude Sucks

> **"Whether you think you can or whether you think you can't, you're right."**
>
> HENRY FORD

When I tell women that I write about dating and relationships, I get lots of comments and questions. After all, dating and relationships are topics everyone can relate to! Some ask me what my next book is about. Others share interesting stories with me. But the response that I get most often? Complaints. Among them: "It sucks to date after forty." "Single mothers have a tougher time dating than single dads." "I'm fed up with men my age [her twenties] because they're all immature." And countless others have complained about men being selfish or about the weird guys they met online.

You may assume these complaints annoy me. They don't; in fact, I encourage them! These women are struggling and I want to know why. If people didn't talk to me, how could I do what I do?

While the frustration these women feel is totally understandable, the real problem they face isn't that dating sucks, or that men suck. It's that *their attitudes* suck. And let me tell you—more than any other mistake I discuss in this book, a sucky attitude about dating or men will single-handedly ruin your dating life. It's that simple. This is why dating success is *largely determined before you ever go on a date.*

I can hear you thinking to yourself, *but my attitude sucks because I've had some really bad experiences!* Yes, bad experiences can sour your attitude, big time. But it also works the other way around: a bad attitude can sour your experiences. Guys can pick up on a woman's bad attitude a mile away. So can the universe. The worse your attitude, the worse your dating life—you won't attract good guys or you won't recognize good guys when they're standing right in front of you.

The types of men and dating situations you attract into your life are directly related to what's going on inside of you. I'll give you an example: throughout my life, when a long and important relationship of mine ends, without fail the next guy I date is an oddball, a jerk, or just totally wrong for me. Even if I have no bad feelings about my ex, my radar and "vibes" are completely jangled due to my loss. Eventually, I end up meeting guys who are better suited for me, but if grief can attract weird guys into my life, imagine what a bad attitude will attract!

And before you think I'm unfairly picking on women's attitudes about dating and men, I'll tell you that men complain to me just as much as women do, if not more. A sucky attitude can happen to any of us if we're not careful.

In this section, you'll learn to recognize the Top Five Bad Attitudes that will destroy your chances of dating success. You'll also learn a bunch of ways to get that attitude back into top shape.

Bad Attitude #1: You Don't Respect Men

Finish the sentence, "Men are _____."

Write down every word you can think of to fill in that blank. Don't over-think it—just write what comes to mind. Once you're finished, look over your list. How many negative words does it contain? If your list contains more than 10 to 20 percent negative words, you may have a problem respecting men. If your list is more than 50 percent negative, you *definitely* don't respect men. If you wrote down derogatory terms like "pigs," "liars," "jerks," "selfish," "sex-obsessed," "dumb," or "shallow," this shows a significant lack of respect for men.

Another sign that you don't respect men is that you don't like being around men socially and prefer the company of women. If you can't fathom spending an evening hanging out with men, you probably don't like them that much. Sure, there are probably some men that you don't want to be around, and that's okay. But if you generally don't enjoy the company of men, it may be a sign that you lack respect for them.

A lack of respect for men can wreak havoc on your dating life in many ways. First, it shows that you don't like men much. Men can pick up on this right away, and they'll run the other way. The first requirement for dating men is *liking* men. You don't have to like all men, or like everything a man does, but you need a general respect for men as a whole. If you don't like or respect men, why should they want to date you? Would you want to date a guy who thinks women are stupid? I hope not!

Another problem is that a lack of respect often means you've had bad experiences with a few men and then have generalized your feelings about those men to all men. However, every man is unique. When women make blanket statements about men, particularly negative ones, men get offended. No man wants to pay for the sins of the men who came before him. If you want to know how this feels, think about a time when you witnessed a man stereotyping women negatively. Perhaps it was a man you dated, or a group of guys you overheard at a bar. And if you've ever read articles or books written for men, some of these "experts" will make broad statements about women, such as:

- Women don't like nice guys
- Women ask what you do for a living because they're trying to find out how much money you make
- Women know they have the power to give or not give sex and will use it to manipulate you

I get annoyed when I hear this stuff because none of these statements have ever applied to me. The men who say these things have bad attitudes. And they have bad attitudes because they've been burned hard by at least one woman. You hate to be lumped in with the bad women these guys dated; likewise, men don't want to be lumped in with the jerks you've dealt with.

A third problem with not respecting men is that, ironically, it will attract men you don't respect into your life. Countless studies have shown that when you believe something (for example, that men are jerks), you will unconsciously look for evidence that men are jerks and ignore evidence that they aren't. In dating, you will choose jerks, not because you want them, but because they seem normal to you. And it works the same way for men. A guy who says all women are bitches wouldn't know a sweetheart if she landed on his lap. He'll choose another bad woman, get burned again, feel more bitter . . . and the cycle will continue.

Being angry at the opposite sex says more about you than it does about men—it tells people that you've failed with men, which doesn't make you look like a catch. Don't be that girl! If you've just been through a breakup or a bad scene with a guy, a bad attitude about men is pretty normal. But the bad attitude should be temporary, and you shouldn't date until that phase is over.

It's true that some men aren't worthy of our respect. But you can choose to avoid these men. If you don't respect men, be sure to read the advice in this section as well as in Mistake #5. Heal the pain you feel over specific men from your past.

Bad Attitude #2:
You Believe the Scarcity Myth

Have you ever made any of these statements?

- "There are no good men left."
- "All the good guys are married or gay."
- "The men in this town are jerks."
- "The men here only want the perfect woman."
- "All the men my age want younger women."
- "There are no good-looking guys here."

If you've made even one of these statements, you've succumbed to the Scarcity Myth. The Scarcity Myth is the very powerful belief that good, available men are extremely hard, if not impossible, to find. The Scarcity Myth is everywhere and can plague women of all ages. Recently I attended a party in my hometown of Denver and spoke to two women around the age of forty. One said that Denver men are unbelievably selfish and all want younger women, and in a separate conversation the other woman said that Denver men, of all ages, are the most quality men she's ever met. These two women are the same age and live in the same city, yet have totally different views on men—one saw good men as scarce, another saw them as plentiful. What's up with that?

Unfortunately, experts can fall victim to The Scarcity Myth too. In her online advice column, one dating expert said that women, especially younger women, too often believe that there are plenty of options and therefore are too choosy with men. Another expert advised a woman living in a major metropolitan city to move to a different city. Why? Because the city she lived in had slightly more single women than men, which the expert felt would hurt this woman's odds.

Women aren't the only ones who fall prey to the Scarcity Myth—some men believe it, too. A couple of years ago, a statistic said that there are more single males than females in Denver. Since then, I've heard numerous Denver men use that as an excuse for not finding a woman. Another Denver guy I know prefers fit women, but said he can never meet one. This region has some of the fittest people in the United States, yet he couldn't manage to find any!

Overall, the Scarcity Myth is just that: A myth. It comes from fear, and it comes from not getting out in the world enough and expanding your circle. If you spend most of your time around married people, men who don't want to marry, or jerks, you will begin to quickly feel like that's all there is in the world, when that isn't the case at all.

Here are a few ways the Scarcity Myth can get you and what to do about it.

Worrying You'll Become a Statistic

When the news cites a new statistic that New York City has more single women than single men, or that the odds of a woman marrying after a certain age are small, it's interesting to watch people let these statistics affect their personal beliefs. But the truth is that these stats, while interesting, have no real effect on your odds of finding love. As someone with a background in statistics, trust me when I say that using stats to calculate your odds of finding a man is totally pointless.

Let's take the number of single women versus the number of single men in a given city. If there are more single women, we're supposed to feel nervous, because our odds of finding a man are supposedly decreased, right? So how does this work? On any given Sunday, do we round up every single man and every single woman and line them up on the streets, match them up, and then tell the women left over, "Sorry, no men for you?" No. The ratio of men to women in any city is totally worthless because you won't meet even a tiny fraction of those men! The only time you should be concerned is if the ratio was more like nine single women for every one single man—and that wouldn't last long, because once single men heard about this amazing city of all women, they'd pack up and move there right away! Remember: all statistics are based on numerous assumptions and limitations. They describe trends, but they cannot determine what will happen in the future.

Another way to worry about numbers is to think quantity is important, that a ballpark of single men to choose from is necessary. Quantity feels good—if you're looking for a black dress, a Giant Black Dress Store would seem great, right? But in reality, you only need one dress, and the Giant Black Dress Store will be filled with a lot of black dresses you wouldn't be caught dead in or don't fit right. A small boutique with five beautiful black dresses could be more helpful. Likewise, what good is a big pool of single guys if most of them aren't right for you? And most of them won't be. What you really want is quality, not quantity.

Worrying about Quality

So if you don't worry about a lack of men out there, you worry about a lack of *good* men out there. Maybe you know there are plenty of guys, but believe they're all "losers," or just wrong for you. This bad attitude is more understand-able than worrying about quantity because finding your type of guy can take a long time. If you date three guys in a row who disappoint you, it can chip away at your attitude. But even though worrying about quality can happen to any of us, it's still a bad attitude you should try to avoid.

The real problem isn't that there are no good men—there are—it's finding a guy who's right for *you*. Unless you get lucky, this takes a lot of time and patience. That's why it's so special when you do find that guy you really click with. As they say, you have to kiss a lot of frogs before you find your prince. Meanwhile, when you meet the wrong guys, whether they're jerks or just not what you're looking for, move on quickly and stay focused on what you want. If you get burned out, take a break.

Worrying about Age

The Scarcity Myth can really hammer women in their thirties, especially if they're approaching forty and still looking to marry. Divorced women over forty can suffer from it too—these women look around and see that a lot of men are already married, that their girlfriends are mar-ried, and even that some men their age are dating younger women! This can be tough.

Fortunately, the Scarcity Myth is no more real for older women than it is for younger ones. Here's why: Women fear that the older they get, the fewer available men there are. If you define available as unmarried, then yes, there are fewer of them. But just because a man is unmarried doesn't mean he's available or right for you. I'll give you an example: I went to college at a school that had nearly 30,000 students. Between classes, going out, and a part-time job, single men were plentiful. Yet, you know how often I found a man I really clicked with? No more often than I do now. These guys weren't married, but some had girlfriends, others were too immature, and still others just weren't my type. More men? Yes. More men for me? No!

The truth is, dating does change when you get older—more men are married, and the single ones are more likely to be divorced, to have children, or even to have commitment issues. The good news is that the men are more experienced, mature, and ready for a relationship. Many women find that dating gets better as they get older. The older you get, the more careful you are about who you date, which means less quantity but more quality. Any cute guy isn't good enough anymore. You have standards that you've had time to develop. By the time you're in your thirties and older, you're much more particular—you're looking for a long-term partner who you're attracted to and who you're compatible with, and most men aren't going to fit those criteria. Overall, everyone—men and women, younger and older—is in the same boat. Everyone wants to find the right partner. The challenge is getting out there, weeding through the wrong ones, and finding that right one.

Overall, if you give in to the Scarcity Myth, it will become a self-fulfilling prophecy—you will lose hope and hurt your chances of finding the guy you want. The Scarcity Myth is based on fear and can make you feel desperate. Fear and desperation don't make you feel, or look, like a catch.

Bad Attitude #3: You're Nursing Old Wounds

For many women, a bad attitude results from having been hurt in the past. When a guy hurts you or breaks your heart, you never forget it. But if you want to find the right guy, you have to let go of the past. Otherwise, you drag your past baggage into your new relationships, probably without even realizing it. Not letting go of old hurts is a very common mistake that causes a lot of problems in a new relationship. If everyone spent more time getting over a breakup or what their ex did to them and less time looking for a new person to make them feel better, relationships would be a lot more successful.

I once dated a guy who complained on a regular basis about the different ways his exes hurt him. Not only did I tire of hearing it, I lost respect for him—not because he'd gotten hurt, but because he held on to the hurt so long and did nothing to let it go. Hurt and disappointment are part of dating, and love. Each relationship teaches you something new and important, and brings you closer to finding the right person.

Bad Attitude #4:
You Complain to Your Friends

Women love to get together and complain about their relationships. And up to a point, this is okay. After all, dating and relationships can be really frustrating and we all need to vent now and again or to get some advice. Otherwise, we'd go insane! But some women make this a hobby. They sit and have coffee or drinks with their friends, tell all their dating war stories, and complain incessantly about men. Nine times out of ten they have no intention of making any changes; they just want to complain. These women don't complain because they're just whiners—they complain because they're good people who want to find the right person, but have faced difficulties and haven't figured out that they have the power to get what they want.

Complaining about problems and not doing anything to fix them, like not respecting men, will attract bad men and bad dating experiences into your life. So it's important to get at the root of your complaint and do something about it. If something bad happens with a guy, tell your friends. Complain. Then, move on.

Bad Attitude #5: You Make No Effort

While some women actively dislike men or believe there are no good men left, other women have a bad attitude in a more subtle way: by not putting forth any effort. Successful dating means taking an active role by choosing the men you want to go out with and helping make the date successful. Passive women expect men to find them, make the first move, make them happy, entertain them, and to do all the right things. These women make little effort and expect men to do all the work.

Take Calli for example. She hasn't had any luck dating lately. She's looking for a relationship but hasn't met any interesting men in a long time. When dating online, she created a profile and posted it, but hadn't actively looked for matches. No men contacted her. When I looked at Calli's profile, it was brief and generic. When I asked Calli why she hadn't gotten more involved, she said she thought she'd done enough.

Calli isn't making a real effort. She put very little effort into the online dating experience, hoping guys would search down her lackluster profile and contact her. Her lack of effort showed and nobody contacted her. Here are some other signs of dating passivity:

Making excuses for your lack of effort. "It's too much work." If you want anything in life, you have to work at it! "Men don't understand my sense of humor." Find one who does! One woman used her Middle Eastern ethnicity as an excuse for why she didn't date. "I'm too ethnic for white guys," she claimed. Hello! Lots of white guys like ethnic women!

Criticizing the date. "He took me to this lame restaurant." "He chose a stupid movie to see." "He talked about himself the entire time." If you don't like his restaurant idea, suggest one of your own. If he talks a lot, jump in the conversation and get yourself heard. Men don't know what you want; you have to tell them. If he's not for you, move on to the next one.

Expecting men to entertain you. Some women go to bars and expect men to buy them drinks simply because they believe men should. The same goes for the free meal idea: "At least I got a free dinner out of it." Just because men will buy you a drink or a meal doesn't mean you should expect it. Never take generosity for granted. This kind of attitude makes you look shallow and like you expect men to do all the work.

You can't sit around and expect a good guy to find you. And while a good guy will put effort into doing things he thinks you'll enjoy, the success of a date is just as much your job as his. The purpose of a date isn't to try new restaurants or critique new movies, it's to get to know each other. If you want to succeed in dating, like anything in life, you have to make a good effort.

The First Step to Cure a Bad Attitude

You've learned that a bad attitude will ruin your dating life. Fortunately, there is a cure for a bad attitude. When you look at the Top Five Bad Attitudes, they all have one thing in common: people that suffer from them aren't taking full responsibility for their happiness. When you don't take full responsibility for your happiness, you become powerless. And when you feel powerless, your attitude suffers. It's that simple.

Taking full responsibility for your happiness means that you're doing everything in your power to get what you want out of dating. It's knowing that you can't control men, what they're like, or how they treat you, but that you can completely control yourself and the choices you make. You control the criteria you have for the men you want, the effort you put into dating, which men you choose to date, whether to keep seeing or dump a guy, and your attitude and mindset about dating. And when things go wrong, you control how to handle them.

Taking responsibility is not the same as taking blame, whether you blame men, dating, or yourself. Taking responsibility is seeing how you can improve things and taking action, regardless of who's to blame. Blame assigns fault, which is a waste of time because you rob yourself of the power to control or change your circumstances. If you blame, something else is controlling you. If you take responsibility, you control you. This is important in dating because so much is out of your control when you date. You can't control whether some dude stands you up for a date.

You can blame him for your bad experience, or you can realize only a loser would stand someone up, and choose to keep looking for a quality man.

So how do you put your new and improved attitude into action? Read on . . .

IF YOU . . .

don't respect men, you can re-think your attitude. Let's say that you're fed up with men who care only about a woman's looks. You can resent men for caring about looks and call them all shallow, or you can take responsibility for your happiness by talking to a variety of men to get an understanding of the looks issue. You can look for men who value who a woman is more than what she looks like. You can improve your own appearance to be more appealing to men, or tone down your appearance so men will focus less on how you look and more on who you are.

believe in the Scarcity Myth, you can consider the facts. Perhaps you're convinced that all the men your age care more about partying than they do about a serious relationship. You can complain that good men are scarce, or you can take a close look at the men you're picking and start paying more attention to the quiet ones rather than going for the loud party guys. You can ask your friends how they meet serious guys. You can look for new ways and new places to meet other kinds of men. You can date men who are a little older.

haven't let go of old hurts, deal with your feelings. Let's say a guy cheated on you. You can resent him for all time and feel like a victim, or you can start by getting counseling to deal with your feelings of betrayal and hurt. You can find books to help you understand why some men cheat. You can learn the signs of a cheater to prevent from getting involved with one again. You can examine your role in his indiscretion—for example, did you ignore the fact that he was a huge flirt or didn't take into consideration that he broke up with his last girlfriend because he was cheating with you?

complain to your friends, consider a more productive plan. Perhaps you're fed up with the flaky men you meet online. You can commiserate with others about the annoyances of online dating, or you can realize that you're not alone and that flaky men are part of dating online. You can enlist your friends to help you devise a strategy to weed the flakes out. You can seek advice from someone who's had success dating online. And when a friend complains about the same issue, you can steer her toward a solution.

are passive, you can take a proactive approach to dating. If you find that you aren't meeting guys, get online and start e-mailing men instead of waiting for them to come to you. Go to places with single people and talk to them. If you find that a man chooses a restaurant or movie that doesn't appeal to you, say you aren't a fan of Indian food or scary movies and politely suggest something else.

Any of us can get a bad attitude when a guy lets us down. It's always a disappointment when a guy doesn't turn out to be what we hoped he'd be. Perhaps he was nice at first and then turned into a jerk. Or maybe he came on strong, like he was very interested, just to suddenly stop calling. Or perhaps you thought he was your type, but it turns out he works too much, watches too much TV, or is too clingy. But no matter how disappointing, blaming and complaining aren't going to solve anything.

The truth is, most of the men you date aren't going to be right for you. That's why a relationship is so special when it does work out. Most people make the mistake of taking this fact of life personally, criticizing and holding a grudge against their date for not being the right one. If you get mad at a man for not being what you want, what good does that do you? How does that get you closer to the right thing? In these situations, the best thing you can do is say "Hey, he wasn't right for me and so I'll keep looking" or "Yuck, what a jerk. I'm going to go find myself a good guy."

Taking responsibility isn't easy. Most of us aren't taught that we have control over our destinies. We're taught that when dating sucks or a guy hurts us, it's his fault, our fault, dating's fault, or the universe's fault. It's hard to see that we play a huge role in our dating and relationship problems. Does that mean we deserve bad treatment or somehow ask for it? Hell no! It just means we choose the guys we get involved with and we choose to stay with them, often because we don't yet realize that we can do better.

Taking responsibility is more than not blaming a guy for disappointing you. It's knowing that you always get to choose, that you always have the power to handle any situation. It's knowing that you can't make a guy do what you want, but you can choose what you do. It's knowing that no matter what a man does—lie, cheat, hit, disappoint—you can choose to leave and find someone better. This doesn't mean you won't hurt, grieve, or feel anger. It means that you can choose better next time.

Strategies to Improve Your Attitude

If you find that you're suffering from a sucky attitude about guys or dating, you've already done the most important thing: realize it. Once you're aware of it, then you can work on changing it. Remember: a bad attitude hurts you way more than it hurts anyone else. Here's how to fix it:

Take Responsibility

The first thing you should do for a bad attitude is take responsibility for your dating life and your happiness. No matter what you've been through and no matter how much you've been hurt, you always have a choice.

This is not to say that the bad experiences you've had with men are your fault; it's that you have the power to choose how you handle such situations, both during the relationship and in the future. If a man treats you badly, you can choose to see that he's a jerk, walk away, and go find a better man. Even if you choose to give him another chance, that's okay as long as you take responsibility for your choice. If he corrects his behavior, great. If not, you don't blame him, or yourself—you choose how to handle it.

Remember You're Not Alone

Dating is hard. There isn't a person in the world who thinks otherwise. Dating makes us face our vulnerabilities. Disappointment and rejection never feel good. Meeting new people isn't that easy. Trying to make conversation with a stranger at dinner is awkward. But anything worth having in life isn't easy or handed to you on a silver platter. You have to work for it. Fortunately, with a good attitude and a little practice, dating gets much easier and more fun.

Avoid Losers

Often, a bad attitude about dating or men starts with spending too much time with jerks, players, or other undesirable guys. Avoid these guys at all costs. Once you see that a guy is a jerk, don't date him. In fact, don't even talk to him. In Mistake #8, you'll learn how to detect jerks and other problem guys more quickly.

Change Your Scenery

A bad attitude is reinforced by the environment you're in most of the time. If you feel like you're the last single woman on earth, stop spending so much time with your married friends and find other singles to hang with. However, if you feel like all men are commitmentphobes, spending a little time with friends who have committed boyfriends or husbands may be what you need. If you're tired of men who party a lot, spend less time at bars and more time in environments that don't involve alcohol.

Rack Up Some Good Experiences

If you've had bad experiences with men or dated a string of undesirables, it will feel like all guys are like that. But they aren't. If going out with a guy doesn't feel good or enjoyable, move on to a different one. It only takes one good guy to erase the bad ones, even if he's a guy you don't wind up with in the long term. Hang out with nice guys, even if at first the only nice guys you can find are your dad or brother.

Get a Good Support System

Gather a network of positive people to talk to when you're feeling bad. During these times, it's helpful to have someone to listen to you, encourage you, and even give you some objective advice. Also, stay away from any friends, family, or even acquaintances with bad attitudes—they'll suck you into their black hole. And avoid anyone who makes you feel worse after you've talked to them.

Let Go of the Past

As you've learned, holding on to negative experiences from your past will negatively influence your dating and your future relationships. If you were hurt by a particular guy, here's a way to release that pain:

1. Write down, in detail, exactly what happened with that guy and how he hurt you. Write down how it made you feel. Be sure to cover all the ways you felt angry, sad, disappointed, and so on. Keep writing until you feel you've said it all.

2. Then, write down what you learned from that bad situation. Include what you learned about him as well as what you learned about yourself and what you want, need, and deserve.

3. Write down how you'd handle the situation if you were in it again. Write down what you'd do differently, and why.

4. Finally, write anything you liked about him or your relationship with him. It may be difficult to recall anything good, but it's important for the healing process.

5. Once you've finished writing, keep what you've written private and/or destroy it. Get rid of anything that reminds you of him or that relationship. Delete any e-mails from him, delete his number from your phone, and destroy or put away any photos.

Here's an example of how this letting-go process works: If a man you loved cheated on you, you could write down exactly what happened and how you found out, as well as any feelings of anger, pain, betrayal, and inadequacy. You might realize that he was a flirt and not ready for a committed relationship, and that if you were in that situation again, you'd break things off once you saw him flirting with another woman. Then, after you've done all that, you might recall that he was fun and made you feel sexy before he cheated. You would get rid of photos of him, and if he calls now and again to see what's up with you, you'd screen his call and never return it.

It's okay to be angry if a man hurts you. It's okay to complain from time to time, and it's okay to feel frustrated about dating now and again. These are normal feelings. No one has a great attitude all the time. The important thing is to take responsibility, focus on the positive, and not let yourself slide into a bad attitude. Focus on what you can do to be happy or what to do better next time. A wise old friend once said to me, "The best revenge is success." If you want to get back at the men who've hurt you, be happy and get what you want out of life.

Mistake #3

You Think Rejection Is about You

> "There is a good way to break up with someone, and it doesn't include a Post-it!"
>
> CARRIE, FROM *SEX AND THE CITY*

If you've ever watched *The Bachelor*, you know that the Bachelor is a handsome, single guy who's looking to settle down. On the show, he meets twenty-five different women and talks with them, takes them on dates, and, over a period of time, eliminates all but one of them. In other words, he has to reject twenty-four women.

It's interesting to watch the different ways the rejected girls react: some look dejected, but hug the Bachelor and say their goodbyes. Others silently seethe, barely hug the Bachelor, and walk off. During the post-rejection interview, some women wish they'd done something different to avoid rejection. Some feel baffled, not understanding why they were rejected. Some express disappointment but accept it. Others feel the Bachelor made a mistake by rejecting them, not realizing how right she was for him. And still others just get pissed, feeling that the Bachelor injured them in some way. *The Bachelor* is a reality show, designed to entertain, but it illustrates the different ways women experience and handle rejection in everyday life.

If you look at all the different ways the women on *The Bachelor* handled the Bachelor's rejection, you'll notice they fall into two categories:

1. Those who accept it wasn't meant to be
2. Those who don't

In your dating life, when you get rejected—and you will at some point—you should be in the first category.

Rejection sucks. I hate it, you hate it, men hate it. There isn't a person in the world who likes being rejected, and rejection will never feel good. But, if you understand what rejection is and why it happens, you can learn to put it in its proper perspective, take it less personally, and not let it screw up your dating life.

I'm going to let you in on a secret. No matter what anyone tells you, there is only ONE reason why a guy rejects you: you aren't right for each other. Think about it: if you go out on a date with a guy you like, and he never calls you after that, you aren't right for each other, at least not at that time. You can't be right for him—if you were, he would have called. He can't be right for you—any guy who's right for you would call you. Yes, my girls, it's that simple.

So how does this work? What factors determine whether two people are right for each other?

What Makes You Hot for a Guy?

Think about the last time you went to an event where there were a lot of men. Perhaps one guy interested you more than others, even before you ever talked to him. Why did he interest you? You could say "Because he was cute," or "Because he dressed nice," or "Because he helped that little old lady with the door." Those reasons make sense. But your two friends, who saw his cuteness, his ironed shirt, and his kindness toward the elderly, did not feel interested in him. You were interested; they weren't. Why?

When we first meet people, we gravitate toward some more than others. This is because they have some quality that we like: perhaps they're attractive, they're interesting, they're similar to us, or they have some quality that reminds us of someone we used to know. We are more attracted to them than to the others, even if in a nonsexual way. Many times, this phenomenon is totally unconscious. We can try to come up with reasons for it, but we can't really control it. This is the most important element of interest and attraction: it is not something we choose.

If you've ever watched *Grey's Anatomy*, you can agree that Patrick Dempsey and Eric Dane, the actors who play McDreamy and McSteamy, are both good-looking guys. Yet, if both guys wanted to go out with me, I'd easily pick Patrick over Eric. No reason other than he just appeals to me more. I can't help it.

Likewise, men too cannot help who they're interested in. What interests or attracts a man may be a little different than what interests or attracts a woman, but the process is still the same—they don't get to choose who interests them. Some women appeal to them, some don't. Some women interest them a little, some a lot. Some interest them at first and then they change their minds. They have no control over this process. And if they can't control how they feel, why should you take it personally?

The Two C's

So what causes interest and attraction? Interest and attraction are really about the two C's: chemistry and compatibility. When you're interested in a guy or find him attractive, you're experiencing chemistry, compatibility, or both.

Chemistry

Chemistry is when a guy just "does it" for you. He looks good to you, he gives you butterflies, makes you nervous, or you just feel excited when he's around. Compared to other guys, he seems special. If he feels the same way around you, it's just a matter of time before a date happens.

When people talk about chemistry, most of the time they're talking about physical or sexual chemistry. But while chemistry may be only physical at first, good chemistry is more than that. Good chemistry with a guy will be intellectual and emotional as well as physical—this is the guy you think is hot AND who you love talking to and being with.

The thing about chemistry is that it's either there or it isn't, and there isn't much you can do to create it with someone. A lack of chemistry with a guy doesn't mean there's something wrong with him, it just means he isn't for you. Likewise, if he doesn't feel chemistry with you, you aren't for him.

Chemistry can be instant, but it can also take a little time to develop. Often, chemistry is the first thing you'll feel when you're interested in a guy, before you've gotten a chance to know him.

Compatibility

Compatibility refers to how well-matched you are with a guy. In other words, he has what you're looking for, and you have what he's looking for. Compatibility is based on a series of different criteria, including:

- Appearance
- Lifestyle
- Personality

- Value system
- Profession
- Goals
- What kind of a relationship he's looking for

Interest and attraction are higher when compatibility is higher. The closer he is to what you want, the better. Likewise, the closer you are to what he wants, the better. Compatibility can range from nonexistent to great, with everything in between. As with chemistry, a lack of compatibility with a guy doesn't have to mean there's something wrong with him, or with you—it just means you aren't a good match.

Often, chemistry creates initial interest in a guy, but compatibility keeps things going. Knowing whether you have truly good compatibility with a guy takes time; however, you can often see a total *lack* of compatibility within the first few dates.

Interest and attraction result from the two C's. If either of the two C's is missing or in low supply, interest and attraction won't be high enough to get a new relationship off the ground. Here are a couple of examples:

Dani met Jake online. They liked each other instantly and their first two dates were great. But by the third date, Dani noticed some differences between her and Jake. Dani is really into fitness and Jake never works out. Dani loves to travel and Jake has never left the United States, and has no desire to. Although Dani still felt attracted to Jake, she started to enjoy his company less. She ended it soon afterward.

Susan met John at a party. Susan instantly liked John—he was funny, outgoing, and polite, all qualities she loves in a man. They talked a lot during the party, and found that they both love the outdoors and live in the same neighborhood. John took Susan out the following week. But even though Susan really liked John, she saw him more as a friend than a potential boyfriend. It bummed her out, but she said no to a second date.

In the first example, Dani felt chemistry with Jake, but there wasn't enough compatibility between them. In the second example, Susan and John had good compatibility, at least so far, but Susan didn't feel enough chemistry. In both cases, the men got rejected—not because there was something wrong with them, but because the two C's weren't there. And in both cases, the women had no choice about how they felt, and had to end things.

This process works the same way with men. If a guy rejects you, he isn't experiencing enough chemistry or compatibility with you at that time. If the chemistry isn't there for him, he can't control that. And if you aren't compatible with what he's looking for, he doesn't have much control over that either. If he's a world traveler who isn't sure he wants kids, he probably won't be into you if you're a homebody who longs to settle down and be a mother. Instead, you would aim for a guy who also wants to settle down and raise a family.

Some people complain that others expect too much compatibility. These people feel rejected when they don't measure up to someone's ideals. For example, Jake might feel annoyed that Dani preferred men who want to travel. But maybe travel is extremely important to Dani. Or, maybe it wasn't the travel itself as much as it was just an overall lack of compatibility between them. The important point is that Dani lost interest in Jake because the compatibility wasn't high enough. It's pointless to make judgments about people's compatibility criteria, no matter how strict or silly they seem. If the feelings aren't there, they aren't there. This is why, when you get rejected, it isn't about you—it's really about the two C's, no matter how personal it feels. With rejection, some aspect of the two C's is missing, and the person who does the rejecting simply figured it out first.

Finally, timing always plays a role in the two C's. People change depending on what life stage they're in and what their needs are at that time. If a guy you're interested in doesn't feel enough chemistry or compatibility now, it's possible he could later, especially if one of the C's is strong.

A Better Way to Handle Rejection

When you date, it's inevitable that you're going to get rejected at some point. No one is immune, no matter how great they are. Understanding the two C's can help you view rejection differently. Think about the different ways you can be rejected:

- He gets your number and then doesn't call
- He makes a date with you and then cancels it, or flakes out
- He takes you out, but doesn't call you after that
- He starts calling you less frequently or acts less interested
- You've gone out a few times and he stops calling altogether
- You call him and he doesn't return your call
- You ask him out and he says no or doesn't follow through

- He tells you he's not interested, or doesn't want to date you anymore
- He hits on or falls for another woman

All the above types of rejection mean the same thing: the two C's aren't there in the right amount. Rejection means "We aren't a good match," not "You're not good enough." Yet despite this, many women come up with all these ways to take rejection personally.

For example, Laurie and Bobby met at a coffee house. Bobby was the best guy Laurie had met in a long time. They went out on several dates, and each time the conversation was great. Laurie could tell Bobby liked her as much as she liked him. Then, Bobby stopped calling. Over a week went by and no call. Laurie felt rejected. She had put on twenty pounds before she met Bobby, and because men she'd known seemed to care so much about weight, she was convinced Bobby had lost interest in her because of that. After two weeks, Bobby called. He apologized for not calling, and explained that he'd run into an ex-girlfriend, and that they had reconciled their differences and gotten back together. Bobby expressed that he'd had genuine feelings for Laurie, and didn't want her to think he'd just lost interest. A few weeks later, Laurie saw Bobby and his girlfriend at a restaurant. Bobby's girlfriend had the same build as Laurie.

Laurie took Bobby's rejection personally. She found an area she felt insecure about and invented it as a reason for her rejection. In reality, Bobby liked Laurie for who she was, including her weight—his girlfriend wasn't skinny either! Fortunately, Laurie got an explanation for Bobby's disappearance, and then got to see his girlfriend. She got to see that her rejection wasn't personal or due to her weaknesses; Bobby felt the two C's with Laurie, but he felt them more strongly with another woman. Most of us won't get this clarity so directly; we just have to believe that it wasn't meant to be.

When you feel rejected, you may find some part of yourself you dislike and blame that. You might ask, "Why isn't he interested?" This is often a pointless question, like asking why he prefers blue over green, or likes his potatoes mashed rather than baked. It's not about your big thighs or the fact that you haven't finished college. That isn't why he rejected you; that's why you reject yourself.

You may also wonder why a guy seemed so interested, then just suddenly stopped being interested. The answer is the same. When you first meet a guy, you don't know how strong the chemistry is or if there's good compatibility. You only know there's enough interest to get things started. Sometimes that initial interest goes somewhere, and sometimes it doesn't. This is why you don't always get a phone call or a second date.

No one likes being rejected. And while rejection will never feel good, at least you can put it into perspective and feel optimistic knowing that you aren't wasting your time with a guy who isn't right for you.

Not Interested, or Just a Jerk?

So far, you've learned about what causes interest and attraction and why you get rejected. The good thing about rejection is that it's a clear message that says, "He's not interested. Move on." But what about those guys who don't directly reject you, but treat you in a rejecting way? Take a look at this list of behaviors:

- He often flakes out on plans with you without good reason
- He says he'll call and then doesn't, then calls at another time
- He flirts with or hits on other women
- He's selfish in bed and doesn't try to please you
- He's rude or disrespectful to you
- He teases you about your flaws

If you experienced any of these signs from a guy you were interested in, what would you think? You might conclude that this dude doesn't like you very much. And, in fact, others might say the same thing, that he's not that interested in you, that he's rejecting you. So what's the deal with this guy—is he experiencing the two C's?

The answer is simple: It doesn't matter. He may feel the two C's, or he may not. Either way, he's a JERK. The best way to handle a jerk is to stop asking yourself if he's interested and start looking for a better guy.

I've noticed a disturbing trend to blame men's bad behavior (which he can control) on a lack of interest (which he cannot control). People, especially men, may tell you he treats you badly because he isn't interested in you or doesn't care about you, when the truth is he treats you badly because he's a jerk. Men who abuse their wives don't do so because they don't care, they do so because they're miserable, insecure human beings. Caring has nothing to do with it. The "right" woman cannot transform a jerk into a gentleman, despite what bullshit Hollywood may tell you. A jerk can change, but not that easily.

As you'll read in Mistake #8, a man who isn't that into you will call less (or not at all) and want to spend less time with you. He will withdraw. But a man who does anything on the above list is a jerk, despite his interest level. When a jerk meets a woman he feels strongly about, he may be on his best behavior and fool her at first, but his true nature will eventually come out.

Remember: how a man treats you reflects the type of person he is, not his feelings for you. Kind, happy men who are successful in life will treat you best, and insecure, unhappy, or unsuccessful men will treat you the worst.

So you've learned why you get rejected and a new way to think about rejection. Now let's move on to more practical matters: the types of rejection, and how to handle it when they happen.

Rejection 101

When you date, there are three types of rejection out there: Good, Typical, and Bad.

A good rejection is when a guy rejects you in an honest and straightforward way. He might say "I just see you as a friend" or "I don't see this going anywhere" or "I've met someone else." He might say it in person, on the phone, or over e-mail, but at least he *says* it. This type of rejection, while not pleasant, is a *gift*. You got the truth, you know where you stand, and you can move on. Unfortunately, good rejection isn't that common.

As you may guess from the name, typical rejection is the most common type of rejection. In a typical rejection scenario, a guy rejects you without actually telling you. Maybe he just stops calling, or doesn't respond if you contact him. If he does tell you the truth, it's only because you asked him directly after he hasn't called in two weeks. These guys are simply afraid of doing it the good way and want to avoid any confrontation or awkwardness, and so they take the easy way out. If you barely know him (he just got your number or you only went out once), the typical rejection makes some sense. Why have a difficult conversation with someone you hardly know? But a typical rejection is more irritating when you've gone out more than once because there's a period of time where you don't know what's happening or where you stand. Just take it as a sign that he's not the guy for you, and move on.

Bad rejection is the hardest to take. With bad rejection, a guy might act like a jerk to you, hoping you'll dump him. He'll disappear without a word after several dates or after sleeping with you. He'll stand you up, make plans for a date and then never follow through, or tell you your flaws when ending things with you. Sometimes, you find out you've been rejected when you see him with another woman. Here's an example of a bad rejection:

Chelsea met Donnie at a party. He asked her out and they had a great time on their first date. He asked her out again, and they went out several more times. During that time, Donnie made moves on Chelsea, even offering to let her stay the night. They fooled around a little but nothing serious happened. After the sixth date, Donnie just stopped calling. After two weeks, Chelsea called Donnie to make sure he'd lost interest and to get closure. Donnie admitted that he'd lost interest.

If Donnie had called or e-mailed Chelsea to tell her he wasn't interested in moving forward, it would have been a good rejection. If he'd stopped calling after one or two dates, it would have been a typical rejection. But after six dates and a little physical intimacy, not communicating to Chelsea put this rejection into the bad category.

Guys who give bad rejections are jerks. If you get a bad rejection, consider it a favor—he let you off the hook so you could go find a man worth being with. Remember:

men who have integrity and feel good about themselves treat others with respect.

Overall, no matter what the type of rejection, it's important to remember that rejection means a guy isn't the one for you. Below, you'll learn how to handle rejection.

Handling Rejection and Disappointment

Rejection and disappointment may be unavoidable when you're dating, but there are ways to make things less awkward and less painful. Employ the following strategies whenever a guy rejects you, and also when you experience disappointments such as a bad date or a guy turning out to be ungentlemanly and rude when he'd seemed polite and sweet.

Strategy #1: Remember he isn't right for you. I've already mentioned this, but it's important enough to mention again. The purpose of dating is to find a guy you want to be with beyond a few dates. Rejection is a clear sign that he is not the guy for you, at least not at that time. Bad rejection or other bad behavior is a very clear sign he isn't the kind of guy you want in your life.

Strategy #2: Know disinterest when you see it. One way to prevent rejection, or at least to head it off at the pass, is to learn to recognize the signs that a guy isn't that interested in you. The more skilled you get at this, the less rejection you have to face because you will see it coming and can stop seeing him, talk to him, or at least be prepared if he rejects you. You'll learn the signs of disinterest in Mistake #8, but overall, this is a guy who doesn't call frequently, doesn't see you frequently, doesn't treat you great, or comes on strong and then backs off. Once you see that a guy isn't listening attentively when you talk to him or that he waits six days to call, you can move on.

Strategy #3: Ask questions. If a guy you've been seeing hasn't called or is acting strange, you can wait to see what he'll do or you can ask him what's up. If he's rejected you, you'll get the truth, which is a lot better than wondering. If he hasn't rejected you, you may feel silly and he may think you're needy, but at least you get the truth. The trick is to ask in a way that seems like you're trying to respect where he's at rather than get mad or upset at him. Sometimes it's as simple as saying, "Is everything okay?" or "Are you having second thoughts about us getting together?" See what he says. If his answer isn't a clear "I like you and everything's great," you may need to rethink him.

Strategy #4: Thank him. Seriously? For rejecting you? Yes, if it's a good rejection. It always better to know the truth. Tell him you appreciate him being honest. This shows you have a solid sense of self and won't fall apart because he rejected you.

Strategy #5: Don't ask why. Because interest and attraction aren't things we choose, asking him why he feels how he does is a waste of time. He might wind up saying something that will make you feel worse. If the two C's aren't there, they aren't there—you don't need to hear that he isn't attracted to you or that he prefers women with a college degree.

Strategy #6: Don't argue. If a guy rejects you or makes excuses (e.g., "I don't have time for a relationship right now" or "I've got a lot to sort out"), don't try to talk him into liking you or talk him out of ending things. If he wants to be with you, or is able to be with you, he would without needing convincing. Your answer should always be, "Thanks for letting me know, and good luck." This shows that you have self-respect and that you respect where he's at.

Strategy #7: Don't be bitchy. Many women make the mistake of getting angry at a guy for rejecting them or not calling them. This only makes you look insecure. Also, because timing is a factor in attraction, being bitchy ruins any chance of things working out in the future. Remember: a guy cannot help how he feels. In the case of a bad rejection, however, a little bitchy might be just what he needs. Your call.

Strategy #8: Consider what you could do better. Although you shouldn't take rejection as an indication of your inadequacies, it can certainly make you aware of them. Sometimes rejection is a good opportunity to improve your game. If you feel that a guy rejected you because you came on too strong, back off a little next time. If you feel that you picked a guy who was a jerk, look for a nicer guy in the future.

Strategy #9: Re-think your own rejection strategy. Although this section is about how to handle rejection, how you handle rejecting guys will directly affect how you handle being rejected—the better you treat the men you reject, the better you'll handle being rejected yourself. In general, when you turn a guy down, you want to be kind, firm, and impersonal. It's not about him; it's about whether he's right for you. You don't owe him a long explanation or specific reasons; just say "I don't think we're a match."

Overall, even though rejection doesn't feel good (and never will), it's important to handle it well. Not only does this make you look (and feel) like a woman who has it together, but it also leaves open the possibility that something could happen in the future. Timing always plays a role in dating, and if the attraction was there to some extent, it could be there later.

Lilly dated Garrett for a few weeks before Garrett started acting a little funny. She sensed that he seemed less interested. Lilly asked Garrett if something was wrong. He admitted that there was, and said he felt that they should just be friends. Lilly had a feeling this was coming and was glad she asked. She felt really hurt, but said okay and was cool about it. Lilly and Garrett managed to remain friends and their paths crossed occasionally. Two years later, when both had matured a little, Garrett became interested in Lilly again.

When Rejection *Is* about You

If you aren't a guy's type or don't have the qualities he's looking for, it feels like it's about you. This is natural, to a point. But it doesn't matter how great you are—you can't possibly appeal to every guy or have what every guy's looking for.

However, there are some situations where it is about you, even if just a little. There are certain dating mistakes women make that most guys don't like, and these can scare off a potentially good guy. You'll learn more about these mistakes in Mistake #5, but here is a quick run-down:

- Moving too fast
- Talking too much
- Talking about the ex or the past
- Always expecting him to pay
- Lying about your age or using old photos online
- Coming on too strong
- Being negative

If you are guilty of any of these and feel they caused a guy to reject you, take the time to work on them.

Years ago, a guy I was acquainted with through my running community e-mailed me and asked me to go white-water rafting with him. He was a nice enough guy, but I didn't feel much interest in him, was casually seeing someone else, and didn't feel comfortable going out with him. So I told him no, and said that I was kind of seeing someone and didn't feel I knew him that well yet. I was very nice in my reply—I wanted him to feel comfortable around me in the future. Unfortunately, my efforts were in vain—he replied back and went on for four paragraphs about how women use the same old excuses, implied that I would have said yes if he'd been better looking or more charming, and complained that he was asking me to do a fun activity, not sit down to a candlelit dinner. He took four paragraphs to say "It bothers me that you said no." He took my rejection, which wasn't at all personal, completely personally, and then punished me for it. I had nothing against this guy—he was nice looking, fit, and friendly. I just didn't feel it. His poor reaction to my saying no made me glad I said no and greatly reduced my opinion of him.

What's my point? Don't let rejection turn you sour like this guy did. Rejection never feels good, but it's part of dating. Looking for a guy you want is like trying to find a good pair of jeans—some will fit badly, some will fit okay but not great, and one or two will fit really well. And while rejection may hurt, it's a good thing in the long run—being rejected is much better than being with the wrong guy, and it shows you that there's someone better out there for you.

Mistake #4

You Have Weak Standards

"The trouble with women
is that they get all excited
about nothing . . . and then
marry him!"

CHER

If asked to describe your ideal guy, what would you say? Perhaps you might say something like, "I want him to be handsome, tall, and athletic. He should be well educated and have a good-paying job, and be between thirty and thirty-five. He should enjoy skiing, love to travel, and want kids." Sounds like a pretty good guy, right? Let's say that, one day, you meet a guy and he's exactly what you described. But after two months of dating him, you break up. Why? It turns out Mr. Ideal works too much, has no sense of humor, and doesn't treat you that great. He looked good on paper, but he didn't make you happy. He wasn't the guy for you.

We've all done this in one way or another. Sometimes the things we think we want turn out to be less important than we thought. Or, we overlook things that are really important because we don't realize how important they are. One of the frustrations of dating is that we look for a guy who's right for us, but more often than not, we don't find him. Why is that?

When you watch your single friends date, what do you see? Do you see that, when looking for men, some of your friends seem to focus on qualities that would be nice but aren't all that important, whereas other friends seem to gravitate toward men who really aren't good enough for them? What is this all about? It's about *standards*. If you want to find the right guy, you need to have good standards. Yet, many women don't—this is Mistake #4.

This section covers the importance of having good standards when you date. However, what should make up those good standards may be a little different than you think.

The Fantasy Man

Maybe your parents read you fairy tales. Perhaps you go see every chick flick that hits the theaters, or secretly read the occasional bodice-ripper. Maybe you've fantasized about Aragorn from *The Lord of the Rings* movie, Brad Pitt, David Beckham, Robert Pattinson, Jamie Foxx, or some other hot guy. Heck, maybe you've fantasized about your doctor, college professor, or boss. Whatever it is, you, like most women, have imagined your Fantasy Man. The Fantasy Man has more influence over your choices in men than you think, and many women have fantasy ideas about love and marriage as a result. However, as you know, the Fantasy Man doesn't exist.

Many people, including experts, will tell you that it's dumb or wrong to have a Fantasy Man. I disagree. Fantasy can tell us a lot about what we really want deep down from men and from life. The trouble only starts when we aren't aware of how our fantasies get in our way, when we confuse fantasy with reality.

For an example, let's start with men. Men have fantasy women. Often, men fantasize about Playboy centerfolds or Victoria's Secret models. To us, it may seem like men have impossible standards, as most women don't look like centerfolds or models. But what these fantasies really mean is that men desire an attractive, sexy woman, which is something any woman can be. However, some men get stuck in their fantasies and only want models or other trophies.

Women fantasize about a lot of different types of men: celebrities, athletes, knights in shining armor. On the surface, it may look like women have impossible standards, that women are too *picky*. But often, when women desire a celebrity, knight, or other Fantasy Man, she's looking for a man who has certain attractive qualities. Do you fantasize about gorgeous celebrities? Perhaps you desire a man who's successful or who cares about his appearance. Do you fantasize about a knight in shining armor? Maybe you're looking for a man who is chivalrous and likes to help others. Fantasize about a rich guy with millions? Maybe you're looking for a financially stable man to give you security. However, as with the men, women can get stuck in these fantasies and have unrealistic expectations of men.

To find the right guy, you have to have realistic expectations. But how do you have realistic expectations without selling yourself short? In dating, you need to have a good set of standards for who you get involved with. To get this good set of standards, you need to know the difference between being picky and being discriminating.

Picky versus Discriminating

"Picky" and "discriminating" sound like similar words, but they have very different meanings. Check out the definitions below, which come from the Merriam-Webster Online dictionary:

Picky: fussy (requiring close attention to details; revealing a sometimes extreme concern for niceties), choosy (fastidiously selective)

Discriminate: to mark or perceive the distinguishing or peculiar features of; to distinguish or differentiate; to make a distinction; to use good judgment

When it comes to choosing the men you date, there's a difference between being picky and being discriminating. If you look at the above dictionary definitions, you can see that "picky" refers to nitpicking and focusing too much on details, whereas to "discriminate" means to look deeper and note the important differences between two things. If you apply this to choosing men, picky means focusing too much on surface characteristics, such as a man's job or height, or on unimportant details such as his decorating style or movie preferences. Discriminating means getting below the surface: how he lives his life, how he treats you, how well-matched he is with you—in other words, discriminating focuses on who a man actually is and how he makes you feel.

Many people confuse picky and discriminating. A discriminating woman might be called picky because she chooses not to date men she knows aren't right for her, even if they're nice or have a lot in common with her. More often, a picky woman describes herself as discriminating, even if that particular word isn't used, if she only wants to date rich guys or doctors, or if she has long list of criteria that she believes are important when they really aren't.

Confusing picky with discriminating will make your dating life frustrating. Have you ever met a really cute guy who was well-educated, had a really good job, and had all the trappings of success, just to find out he's a total bore, or worse, a total jerk? Confusing picky with discriminating can also negatively impact your future. How many couples do you know who are unhappily married, not because they're having normal marital problems, but because they're a terrible match for each other? If they'd been more discriminating, or less picky, they may have prevented a bad marriage, or a divorce and all the problems that come with it.

Are You Ms. Picky?

When it comes to choosing men, women can be picky about many things—too many things to list here. However, there are a few key areas that many women tend to focus on. In this section, we'll take a closer look at what those are.

Occupation

Occupation is the top item women are too picky about. Even independent, thoughtful women fall prey to focusing too much on a man's job title. One reason for this is that occupation is an indicator of status and high-status men attract women by the boatload. Occupation is also an indicator of income. However, while occupation can certainly tell you a lot about a man, it isn't always a good indicator of his income, and it's a lousy indicator of his ability to treat you well or to make you happy. How many times have you written a guy off because his occupation wasn't impressive to you? One woman dated a bartender a couple of times, but then broke it off. "He's a bartender," she said, "I can't see this going anywhere." What does being a bartender tell this woman about this guy's ability to be a good partner? Not much.

Here are some occupations women tend to admire:

Doctors, CEOs, and other high-status jobs. Medicine is a noble profession, and you have to be bright and dedicated to get into med school, much less get through it. Running your own shop as a CEO takes courage and leadership skills. However, there are many other occupations that require those characteristics. And just because he's dedicated or gutsy doesn't guarantee he'll treat you right.

Musicians, actors, and other creative types. Musicians and actors have become high-status in our culture, which is why they attract so many groupies. Perhaps seeing a man do something creative is sexy. Creativity, and the love of it, is an important value for some of you. That's fine. Just be sure to look at everything he is, beyond his craft.

Don't get me wrong; it's okay to like doctors, musicians, or men in any occupation that turns you on. All I'm saying is that when picking a partner, you shouldn't give more credence to these guys than to ones working in other fields. Judge a man by who he is and how he treats you, not just what he does for a living.

A lot of what attracts us to a given occupation is our perception of that job and what sort of man would do it. This is why doctors and musicians are Fantasy Men for a lot of women. Spend some time thinking about what these occupations mean for you, and what you imagine these men have going for them. Then, look for men who have those qualities.

Income

Many men believe that a man's income is the only thing that matters to women. These men are fools. However, their beliefs don't come totally out of the blue—while women care about much more than a man's wallet, many still care about the wallet more than they should. Today, women aren't as concerned about income as they used to be because they have careers of their own. However, many women still desire high-income men because they want the comforts that come with money and aren't able or willing to earn enough themselves. Yet, like occupation, money doesn't tell you what kind of man he is or how he'll treat you.

Judging a man by his income is no different than him judging you by your looks—you're more than your face or boobs, right? Well, men are more than their wallets. There isn't a person in the world who wouldn't mind having more cash, or mind dating someone who has it. And there's nothing wrong with wanting a man to have a respectable job with a decent income. But lots of money, and the comforts that come with it, are a bad substitute for happiness with your soul mate.

Height

Women care about how tall a guy is. While this is fine, some women put more emphasis on stature than is necessary. To see what I'm talking about, visit a large dating website and see what qualities women look for in men. In my research, I noticed an interesting pattern with the women—whatever height these women were, many wanted a man at least five inches taller than they were, if not more. This pattern was so common that I labeled it "The Five-Inch Rule."

I know many of you have this fantasy of a big, strong man. But really, does a big strong man have to tower over you? Are you really going to wear ankle-busting heels every time you're with him? Good men come in all heights. And by wanting men who are much taller than yourself, you're not only ruling out a *lot* of men, you're ruling out a lot of *good* men.

> Amy, who's five feet nine, has always preferred tall men. She required any man she dates to stand over six feet, so she could feel petite. So she dated tall men, and ignored "short" men—i.e., any man less than six feet tall. None of the tall dudes ended up working out. Eventually, Amy met a great guy and fell in love. He treated her like a queen. This great guy? Five foot ten. Barely taller than her. Her height requirement? Out the window.

Height does not define a man—his confidence in himself does. I would never suggest that you date a man you aren't attracted to. All I'm saying is give men of all heights a chance. The man who really makes you happy may not look the way you thought he would look, but you'll be wildly attracted to him anyway.

Education

Many women prefer men who have a college education or who've gone to professional school to get their law or medical degrees. To some extent, this is understandable. Education gives us skills and a broader view of the world, and educated men tend to be more accomplished. However, many people put more importance on education than they should.

First, a college degree doesn't necessarily mean he's smart—the hard part about getting through college isn't the intellectual challenge so much as the financial challenge, and for all you know, his parents footed the bill. Also, a college degree doesn't necessarily mean he's going somewhere in life—if you've ever spent time on a college campus, you know that some guys spend more time getting hammered than learning anything. Finally, we live in a country where anybody can succeed—many successful businessmen and millionaires never even went to college.

My point is this: don't place too much emphasis on a college diploma. As with all other superficial traits, look beyond what's on paper to see what kind of person he is.

Age

Many women have a strict age range when it comes to men. And this range is unlikely to include younger men. Many women automatically rule out men who are younger than themselves because they assume younger men lack the very things women want: maturity, accomplishment, and a desire to commit. To some extent, this makes sense—men typically mature more slowly than women do, so we assume that a man who's younger than us can't cut it. Sometimes this is true, but sometimes it's not, and you're ruling out a lot of potential soul mates by ruling out younger guys. Besides, older men aren't always mature!

This advice is especially important as you get older. If you're twenty-seven, dating a younger man might be tougher because men under twenty-five are less likely to have the maturity you need. But if you're in your thirties or older you'll find that some men over twenty-five, and certainly men over thirty, are often mature and accomplished enough and may have what you're looking for.

I'm not suggesting that you shouldn't care about occupation, income, height, education, or age. I'm only saying that if you want to find the right man for you, don't automatically accept men, or rule them out, based on these five things. Look deeper.

The Importance of Discrimination

If I had to give you one piece of advice, I would tell you to be very discriminating when you date, especially if you're looking for a long-term relationship or marriage. A lot of relationships and marriages suffer because the people involved weren't discriminating enough when they were still dating. Being discriminating means knowing what sort of man you want to be with and what sort of relationship you need, and not dating men who don't fit that standard. This is about more than avoiding abusive men or men who drink their body weight in beer every week; it's about avoiding men who aren't right for you, even if you like them. The trick is to focus on who a man really is deep down, and how he makes you feel.

Most of us weren't taught to be discriminating. The ability to discriminate and choose men who are good for you is a skill that will develop with experience. And the more experienced you are, the quicker you can do this.

Being discriminating makes dating much easier and more efficient. Once you figure out what you want, you can stop dating men who don't have what you want and focus on the few who do. Dating is about more than attracting men; it's about picking men, and picking the right men.

A good way to show you what being discriminating looks like is to give you some examples of what a *lack* of discrimination looks like. Here are several examples of low discrimination:

- Dating a guy you don't have much in common with because he's cute or makes a lot of money
- Dating a guy you have a ton in common with but with whom you feel little chemistry
- Dating a guy you know isn't right for you because you're bored or lonely
- Continuing to see a guy who's shown flaky behavior, such as canceling a date at the last minute (without a very good reason) or not calling when he said he would
- Continuing to date a guy who's seeing other women, when you want exclusivity
- Continuing to date a guy who isn't showing genuine signs of interest in you
- Dating a guy who treats you poorly in any way
- Dating a guy who doesn't meet your must-have requirements
- Dating guys who have wives or girlfriends, or who are otherwise unavailable

Another word for not being discriminating is *settling*. Settling is accepting less than what you really need in a relationship. Many people think settling is dating someone who doesn't have every picky thing you want, but it's actually dating someone who's a bad match for you or who doesn't treat you right. Ironically, being picky can lead to settling. When you're too picky, you don't get what you really need, and eventually you give up and settle.

Society loves to pressure people, especially women, to settle. Some people will give you grief for breaking up with a guy you feel weak chemistry with or who doesn't treat you right. Also, the pressure to marry causes many women to settle. So does the pressure to have children before the baby factory retires. So does inexperience, desperation, loneliness, and poor self-esteem. This is why it's so important to know what you need in a relationship, and to avoid those who can't give it to you, even if that means dating less often.

> Ashley is thirty, pretty, and successful in her career. She's ready to settle down with a man, get married, and start a family. When she dates, she always aims for the same type of guy: very handsome, confident, and with a high-status job. When she meets her Mr. Handsome, they date and get involved, but invariably things don't work out. These guys always wind up blowing her off, treating her with disdain, or cheating on her. Ashley's problem is that when she picks guys, she's picky but not discriminating. She focuses only on a man's looks and status and doesn't factor in how well-matched they are or how he treats her. Currently, Ashley is still looking for Mr. Right.

Putting It All Together

If you think about picky and discriminating together, you'll see more clearly how they apply to dating.

Discriminating	Not Discriminating
Picky	
Nitpicky, fault-finding, and judgmental	Cares primarily about looks, status, or money
Relationships are few and far between	Relationships seem good at first but aren't satisfying in the long term
Seek Mr. Perfect	Seek Mr. High Status
Example: The commitmentphobe who can never meet the right guy	Example: a woman who only dates handsome doctors
Not Picky	
Focused on chemistry and compatibility	Low standards, low self-esteem, or inexperienced
Relationships more likely to be successful over time	Relationships unsatisfying
Seek Mr. Right	Seek Mr. Right Now
Example: a woman who picks men who are well-matched for her	Example: any woman in a relationship with a man who treats her poorly

The table above illustrates this point by showing you how women date and the types of men they seek based on how picky and discriminating they are.

It isn't just women who have trouble with picky versus discriminating. Although most men aren't as picky as women are, they too make mistakes in this area. For men, pickiness almost always revolves around women's looks. Picky men always want the hot chick. Most of the time, these guys aren't very discriminating and don't use good judgment in choosing a date or partner because they're caught up in looks. Here's how picky and discriminating look in men:

Discriminating	Not Discriminating
Picky	
Find flaws in every woman	Seek hot women, trophy wives, or much younger women
Bad at getting close to women	Choose women who aren't good matches for them
Common in: men who can't commit, men who have issues about women	Common in: younger men, wealthy/successful men
Example: Jerry from *Seinfeld*	Example: Most of Patti's clients on *Millionaire Matchmaker*
Not Picky	
Want more than physical beauty	Have low standards
Want a partner and friend	Often young, inexperienced, immature, or out of practice
Common in: experienced men, highly educated men	Common in: Players, younger men, men on the rebound
Example: Ross from *Friends*	Example: Joey from *Friends*

With maturity and experience, men can learn to choose better partners. And so can you. In the next section, you'll put these concepts into practice by making a checklist.

Making the Checklist

In order to avoid settling for less than what you really want, you have to be clear about what you really want. You need a checklist of items you want in a potential partner. All possible checklist items are too numerous to list here, but here are some things to consider:

HIS:

- **Appearance:** e.g., build, coloring, personal style
- **Personality:** e.g., serious or goofy, Type A or laid back
- **Lifestyle:** e.g., eating, drinking/drugs, hobbies, how he spends his free time
- **Profession:** e.g., education, field of work, job, work ethic
- **Finances:** e.g., income, financial responsibility, spending habits
- **Values:** e.g., religious beliefs, political and social stances, cultural identity
- **Baggage:** e.g., marital history, kids, family and personal history
- **Goals:** e.g., personal goals, financial and professional aspirations

The above list includes things most people consider when looking for a partner. However, there are a few other crucial items that many people overlook:

Your overall opinion about him. Do you respect him? Do you admire his accomplishments or his progress in life? Are you proud to introduce him to your friends or family?

How you feel when you're with him. Does he make you laugh? Does he make you think? Do you feel relaxed with him? Do you enjoy his company?

How he treats you. Is he respectful? Kind? Does he listen? Help you do the dishes? Call when he says he will? Compliment you? Comfort you when you cry? The handsome, successful, masculine guy is totally worthless if he doesn't treat you well.

His relationship style. Is he romantic or pragmatic? Is he affectionate or more reserved? Does he like to spend a lot of time together, or need more space? Is he communicative or harder to read?

The relationship he wants. Does he want casual dating, a relationship, or marriage? This is probably the most overlooked item in dating and causes many problems in dating and relationships, often because one or both parties become emotionally involved before realizing that the other doesn't want what they want. Also, does he want kids? Overall, does he want what you want?

The checklist can be as long as you want, and you can put whatever you want on it. However, there are two more things to consider when making your checklist: One, every checklist needs to differentiate what you'd like from what you *must have*. You may like tall men, but you may find you don't *have* to have one. Knowing a desirable trait versus a must-have comes from experience. Must-haves are not negotiable; you can evaluate everything else on a case-by-case basis.

Two, every checklist is a work in progress. It can and should evolve as you learn more about yourself and what's really important to you. Sometimes you'll meet a guy who doesn't fit your standards in some way, but you like him anyway. For example, you prefer educated guys and then meet a great guy who hasn't finished college. Date him, see if the college thing is that important, and alter your checklist if necessary.

How to Date with High Standards

Once you've constructed your checklist, here are some pointers to help keep your standards high when you date:

Memorize your checklist. Put some time into making a detailed checklist. Then, review it on a regular basis to keep in mind what you want and to make any revisions to it. This will greatly increase your odds of meeting men who have what you want.

Abide by your must-haves. Don't date men who don't have your must-have items, no matter how lonely, bored, or horny you are. Why waste time with the wrong guys? If you choose to break this rule, pay attention to how things go. If they go well, maybe it's time to revise your checklist. If they go badly, it will reinforce the importance of that item.

Focus less on picky stuff. Focusing too much on surface traits won't get you a happy relationship. Many women think they want a tall guy or a rich guy, and then find that they're perfectly happy with a shorter guy or a guy who makes a regular income. While it's okay to have picky items on your checklist, limit the number of these items that are must-haves.

Road test your picky stuff. To find out whether a picky item is an ideal or must-have, road test it—date a guy who you like and who has other traits you want, but is missing some trait you think is important to you. Then, see what happens. You may decide your instincts were right and that education (or height, age, and so on) really is that important to you. Or, you may be pleasantly surprised to find that this "compromise" isn't a compromise after all. Personally, I don't care much about income, education, or height, but my guy must be physically fit. I've road-tested this one, and can't live without it.

Don't settle. Sometimes it's easy to get caught up in picky items and forget to evaluate how well-matched you are, how a guy makes you feel, or how good the chemistry is. For example, you may meet a great guy and then find that he isn't interested in getting married. To stay with him would be settling. Don't date guys who don't fit your criteria. Dating with discrimination means you'll date less often; however, the dates you do go on will have better potential. Hold out for better—many women date the wrong guys because they've never had something better. Once you know you can get better, you won't settle for less.

Do the Fantasy Man exercise. Take some time and write down who your Fantasy Man is. What does he look like? What are his personality traits? How does he treat you? Include every detail you can possibly think of. Then, look at what you've written. Do you notice any themes in your description? Is he physically attractive to you? Is he a go-getter who's successful? Is he romantic and affectionate? Write down why you like those things. Whatever he is, these are things that are important to you. Although the Fantasy Man doesn't exist, he can show you what's most important to you in a man.

The Online Fantasy

If you've ever experienced the world of online dating, you're aware of its numerous benefits and challenges. One challenge you may not have considered is that dating online strongly encourages pickiness and makes discrimination more difficult.

Online daters often suffer from "Design-Your-Ideal-Mate Syndrome." Dating sites allow you to select on very specific traits such as hair and eye color, height, weight, education, and income before you even meet anyone. This is problematic. Who's to say that the cute guy with blonde hair, blue eyes, a master's degree, and an interest in the outdoors won't turn out to be flaky, negative, and a slacker? Check out these two examples of women who didn't use online dating to their benefit:

Jaclyn decided to start dating online to increase her chances of finding a good guy. When selecting her search criteria on the dating website, she selected men her age or a little older, over six feet tall, living no more than a few miles away, and with an income higher than hers. She submitted her search criteria, and out of thousands of men, only three fit those criteria. Renee joined a large dating site, did her searches, went out with a few men who met her criteria, and had no luck at all. Soon after, she went to a friend's barbecue and met a great, cute guy. They hit it off, started dating, and eventually got married. During their dating phase, they both realized they'd been on the same dating site at the same time, and had not shown up in each other's searches. Why? She'd searched on men who were over six feet (he was 5'10"), and he'd searched on women his age or younger (she was two years older than him).

Jaclyn suffered from Design-Your-Ideal-Mate Syndrome. Yes, ideally her guy would be her age, but why rule out men who are only a couple of years younger? Unless you're nineteen, those few years aren't going to matter. She wanted men over six feet, but she's only 5'8", so why wouldn't 5'10" or 5'11" work? Why couldn't she drive more than a few miles to be with the man of her dreams? And he couldn't make a little less money than she does?

Renee, although not as picky as Jaclyn, almost missed out on finding her husband because of a height criterion that didn't matter. And her guy almost did the same thing with her; again, for an age criterion that wasn't important!

Another challenge is that it's tough to be discriminating online because you don't get a good feel for a guy until you meet him, increasing your chances of meeting a total jerk. Here are a few pointers to help you weed out men who aren't worth your time:

Carefully read his profile: You can get a good idea of a man's character from reading his profile. Avoid men who say negative things, no matter how much you agree with them (e.g., he hates Republicans). Be wary of guys who have poorly written or sloppy profiles. And steer clear of men who don't post photos—it means they probably have something to hide. This is a common way married men troll for women to sleep with, and it just isn't safe.

When they express interest in you: Look for men who address you politely. They should greet you by your name or by the handle you've chosen. They should show interest in you and comment on something you've said in your profile. Avoid men who make silly comments, sexual remarks, or who seem like they don't take the process seriously.

When you're in contact: A man should be fairly prompt in his responses. If he takes more than three days, he may not be that interested, or just flaky. If he isn't reliable over e-mail, he won't be reliable in real life. If he asks to meet you, he should respect your safety and suggest a public place for you to meet. Blow off any man who is anything but polite and respectful. You should feel comfortable meeting him. Always trust your instincts— if something doesn't feel right, for any reason, don't bother.

Online dating can be a great way to meet someone. But, you have to approach it differently than traditional dating. Tone down the pickiness and try to discriminate as much as possible before you meet a man in person. You'll meet a lot of men who aren't right for you, but you may meet someone special.

Overall, everyone, male or female, wants the same thing—a partner who we're attracted to and who we really click well with. In your fantasies, you may imagine you'd click well with a gorgeous guy or a doctor. But in reality, who you wind up clicking with is rarely who you've imagined. Keep an open mind and don't rule out men on surface characteristics. Rule them out because they aren't right for you.

Mistake #5

You Don't Get Men

> **"Women mistakenly expect men to feel, communicate, and respond the way women do."**
>
> JOHN GRAY, IN *MARS AND VENUS ON A DATE*

In an online dating column, a woman asked for suggestions on how to charm a man or make him feel good. "Send him flowers," she was advised by the female "expert." "Men rarely receive flowers." Of course, men are much more than meat-eating cave dwellers. But have you ever met a man who put "flowers" high on his list of things that make him feel special? This expert didn't quite get men.

If you've ever worked in sales or in an industry that sells any type of product, you know that the better you understand your customer, the more likely you are to make a sale. Well, it works the same way in dating. To some extent, when we date, we're "selling" ourselves to guys, and they're selling themselves to us. Just like men who understand women have better luck dating, women who understand men well tend to have a lot of loyal men vying for their company.

How well do you understand guys? If you ask the average man how well he understands women, he will probably admit he doesn't understand them that well. But if you ask women how well they understand men, many will claim to understand men pretty well. Yet, if this were the case, men wouldn't complain to me! The truth is, most women could stand to understand men better than they do. The more you understand men, especially the ways they approach dating, the more success you'll have dating them.

This section will discuss what you need to know about men when you date. You don't need to know all there is or understand men completely. The important thing is to have a good understanding of how men approach dating, and to try to see things from their point of view and not just your own.

There are many ways to misunderstand men, but most of them fall into the following four categories:

"Come On, Men Aren't That Different."

Some women don't realize that men are different in some key ways. They're the ones who assume that because they like something, men will like it too. For example, on a date a woman goes into great detail about the big sale at J. Crew because that's something she and her girlfriends find interesting. Not realizing that men are different is usually due to inexperience.

If you don't understand the ways men approach dating differently, it can hinder your dating success. For example, men ask women out and women wait to be asked. This isn't iron-clad, and asking a man out is fine in certain situations, but most of the time men do the asking. The tendency for men to pursue women in this way is biological, so when you've shown your interest and he isn't asking, there's usually a reason. Women who don't realize men are different in this way wind up chasing men who aren't interested or available.

Another example is that many men can have sex with women they aren't interested in beyond sex, whereas most women are interested in the men they have sex with. Again, this difference isn't iron-clad, but it's true more often than not. Women who don't realize this may feel hurt when a man they like only wants sex and not a relationship. You'll learn more about this key difference later in the section.

Once you learn the basic differences between men and women, you will date with more success.

"Men Are SO Different, I Can't Even Deal."

Instead of assuming men are the same as women, women in this mindset go to the other extreme and assume men and women are polar opposites. They know men are different than women, and often make sweeping statements about both sexes. Many see men as a different species entirely; "It's like we're from different planets," they'll say. When women say something like this, they've probably had difficulties with men. After all, a lack of understanding between different groups of people will create conflict between them. This type of thinking can also be the result of being raised in a home where Mom and Dad had traditional roles and raised the boys differently than the girls.

Women in this category tend to see male-female differences in black and white terms and refuse to see any commonality. For example, a woman in this category will state that men care about sex while women care about romance, not acknowledging that both sexes care about both, even if in different ways.

The problem with this kind of thinking is that it creates a gulf between you and the men you date. It focuses on the differences instead of how to understand or handle the differences. This section will discuss these differences and how to handle them, and suggest ways to see things from men's point of view. Until you can see that men are human and have many similar needs to us, you will struggle with dating.

"All Men Are . . ."

Everybody stereotypes. And dating is no exception; women have stereotyped ideas of men, men have stereotyped ideas of women, and dating advice books and columns have stereotyped ideas about both sexes. Why is that? Human behavior, including dating behavior, is very complex and not always predictable or easy to understand. Stereotyping is a tool people use to gain a basic understanding of what is complicated. It's a good thing, to a point. The problem comes when we forget that a stereotype is a simplification— it is part of the truth but not the whole truth.

Stereotyping takes behaviors commonly seen in men and creates a "type" that applies to all men, all the time. Stereotypes oversimplify complex behaviors and put them into a simple package—for example, "Men like sex and women like romance" or "Men think with their dicks." The problem with stereotyping is that most men don't fit stereotype molds. Some men like romance; other men, not so much. Also, it's very trendy these days to refer to men as "simple creatures." Men will say it, women will say it, experts will say it. Men may be simpler to understand than women, but they aren't simple. They may have certain tendencies, but every man is unique. Not every man will have every "typical" male trait, and the ones who do will have it to different degrees. You'll read some specific examples of this in the next section.

You've probably experienced your own frustrations with stereotypes. For example, a guy friend or dating expert says, "Women aren't attracted to nice guys." How does that make you feel if you love nice guys? "Women prefer romantic movies," they'll say. Sure, *Pride and Prejudice* is a favorite of mine, but it sits on my shelf between *Kill Bill* and *Tommy Boy*. We don't fit every stereotype for women, so why would men fit all the male stereotypes?

Beware of stereotypes. To a point, they can help you understand men. Just remember that men come in all shapes and sizes and that stereotypes can only tell you so much.

"I Know How Men Are—I've Had Three Boyfriends!"

Most of our beliefs and impressions of men come from our personal experiences. It starts with our fathers and continues with the guys we get involved with. If the men we've associated with are jerks, then we conclude all men are jerks. If they're unfaithful, we assume all men are easily tempted. A lot of women don't realize they generalize like this. Then they excuse their beliefs by saying, "Hey, in my experience, this is how men are. And all my friends have had the same experiences!" The problem with this kind of thinking is that it becomes a self-fulfilling prophecy. And it will scare off any good guys!

While our beliefs about men are based on our experiences, it works the other way around too—our experiences are based on our beliefs. If we believe men are jerks, those are the men we will attract. Some call this phenomenon the "law of attraction," which is well-documented in books like *The Secret*. This phenomenon has also been demonstrated over and over in psychological experiments. When people have a certain belief, they will look for examples to support their belief and ignore those that don't. They don't even realize they're doing it. If you've been with unfaithful men, you'll look around and find examples of married men checking out other women and overlook those who aren't. Then, you attract more men like that because your attention is on them. And because that's how you see the world, you will attract friends who are like yourself and have the same experiences as you, reinforcing your beliefs. It's a vicious cycle.

Dating experts can fall victim to this as well. Have you ever noticed how advice from one expert can differ so much from the advice of another expert? One reason for this is that they see the world differently based on their own experiences and beliefs. One female expert feels strongly that all men are players at heart and that a woman should be very challenging to keep men interested. She advises women to expect a man to pay for everything (he won't respect you if you contribute) and to withhold sex for a very long period of time (he won't respect you if you have sex too soon). This expert admits that her father was a major womanizer—knowing this, her advice isn't that surprising. She's probably a good expert on how to date players, but not necessarily on how to date normal men.

In the field of behavioral research, we're interested in patterns of behavior, not the behavior of one or two individuals. If we want to study men, we wouldn't interview one, two, or even twenty men—we'd interview hundreds of men of varying backgrounds. The same is true for you. If you want to truly get men, you have look beyond your experiences. If you want to succeed in dating, you have to be aware of how your experiences have influenced how you see men and the men you choose to date.

Overall, remember that our view of men is based on our unique experiences and belief systems. Examine your past relationships with men, including your father and your former boyfriends. Do you see any negative patterns? Is there a pattern of abuse, womanizing, emotional unavailability? Were they possessive, workaholics, spineless? The key is to be aware of your unique dating patterns and know that there are other options. There are men who will never cheat, who know how to love, who know how to cook, or who otherwise don't fit your idea of what all men are.

Men: Stereotypes Versus Truth

In the previous section, you learned about stereotyping men and women's tendency to see men a certain way. Stereotypical ideas about men can come from our experiences, but they're also strongly perpetuated by TV, movies, dating books, and even by men themselves. Stereotyping makes for great comedy, but it's not so great when you're dating. You can't believe stereotypes and get men at the same time.

Here is a list of common male stereotypes, followed by the research-based truth about each one.

Stereotype: Men think with their dicks.

Truth: Men perpetuate this stereotype even more than women do—countless comedy routines are based on this premise alone. Sure, a horny guy isn't the most rational creature on earth, and he'll think of everything in terms of sex. But women also make bad decisions when they need sex (why do you think there are so many unwanted pregnancies?). Men aren't always horny, despite what they say—men's sex drives vary considerably depending on their personality, their age, and whether they're getting sex regularly. And men have the ability to rein it in. Most men who date are interested in more than sex, and most have no problem being faithful.

Stereotype: Men won't respect you if you sleep with them too soon.

Truth: Some men have Victorian views about women. That's their choice. But many men don't have a number of days or dates a woman should wait to have sex with him. Most men know when the time is right, just like you do. And respect is something you have for yourself, not something bestowed on you by men. Most men respect women who respect themselves and have sex when they're ready to. If a guy likes you, he'll stick around, regardless of when you first sleep together. And, of course, we've all met those long-time couples who slept together on their first date.

Stereotype: Men are threatened by powerful or successful women.

Truth: Some men are. It isn't your success that's the problem; it's their insecurity about their own success (or lack of it). Fortunately, many men are impressed by successful women, especially if these men are accomplished themselves. However, men are turned off by the arrogance and competitiveness that comes with some successful women. Men need to feel appreciated and like they measure up to their partner's standards.

Stereotype: Men love porn.

Truth: Most men have looked at porn at some point during their lives, and most aren't opposed to watching it. But there are a lot of men who don't seek it out or just aren't that interested in it, especially if they're getting the real thing. If you don't like porn or even *Playboy*, don't let anyone tell you to put up with a guy who looks at online porn or keeps stacks of nudie magazines around the house. There are plenty of men who don't care that much about it.

Stereotype: Men like sex, not romance.

Truth: Men like both. Most men don't flock to romance the same way women do, but they value it more than you think. They just don't want to admit it because they don't want to appear too "soft." However, men vary widely in this area; some men always remember anniversaries and birthdays and want to do something special, but other men have to be reminded and pushed to do these things.

Stereotype: Men just want to "spread their seed" and don't want monogamy.

Truth: People who believe this stereotype are typically players or women who've been with unfaithful men. Men are biologically designed to spread seed, and can if necessary, but they're also wired for monogamy. Monogamy ensures that children survive and are raised properly. Most men want monogamy once they're ready. If they didn't, it wouldn't be so widespread! If you don't believe me, look around. Most men, across the world and throughout history, stick with one woman at a time.

Stereotype: Men fear commitment.

Truth: Most men will commit when they're ready, whether that commitment is to be exclusive, to move in together, or to get married. They'll do this without being pushed or nagged. Men perpetuate this stereotype just as often as women. If a guy tells you men fear commitment, that means HE fears commitment. Statistically, over 90 percent of men in the United States marry at some point, most of those by the age of forty. If men feared commitment that much, that number would be much lower. However, it is true that, on average, men take longer than women do before they're ready for marriage. And they're less likely than women to jump into a commitment they aren't ready for. Commitment is a big deal, so a little fear is a good thing. But most men won't let their fears stop them.

Stereotype: Men prefer younger women.

Truth: Most men seek out women close to their age, and most couples are close in age. This makes sense—similar-aged couples have more in common and relate to each other better. However, if men are going to deviate from the norm, they will more often choose a younger woman over an older woman. One explanation for this is evolutionary theory: a young, fertile female can produce children and the older male can provide and care for her and the children, making sure the species doesn't die out. This is also a reason why women tend to choose older men over younger men.

However, while humans are driven by the need to reproduce (i.e., by sex), we're driven by more than that. We want love. We want a partner to share our lives with. This is why older man-younger woman relationships, which are less likely to be compatible partnerships, aren't the norm. This is also why older woman-younger man relationships, which don't make sense from an evolutionary standpoint, exist and have become more common. Many older men may find younger women attractive physically, but physical attraction alone won't keep a relationship together long. Smart and/or experienced men know this and don't chase younger women.

Stereotype: Men care most about looks and prefer hot women.

Truth: Some experts (especially if male) will push this stereotype. However, while men do notice looks first, most men place as much or more value on other traits such as intelligence, personality, and self-confidence. And while men admire hot women, that doesn't mean they expect their partner to look like a model. As you learned in Mistake #4, beautiful women are fantasies to men like cute doctors or musicians are to women. Great looks will catch a man, but they won't keep his interest —a relationship will not survive on physical attraction alone.

Many younger men (teens and early twenties) fit this stereotype. But once they catch a beauty and realize she's a human being with flaws, that he has nothing in common with her, or worse, that she's bitchy or crazy, they learn their lesson. Some men never learn and continue to chase "tens" into old age! Just as importantly, chasing isn't getting: research shows that if you use a one-to-ten rating system for attractiveness, the vast majority of couples are within a point or two of each other.

Stereotype: Men are visual, women are emotional.

Truth: This is easily the most misused statement about male-female differences. It is used in dating (e.g., men notice a woman's looks and women focus on how a man makes her feel). It is also used with sex (e.g., men like porn and lingerie, women like romance novels and romantic gestures before sex). You can see some of the truth in this stereotype, but it is a gross oversimplification. Women are visual, too—they care very much about how a man looks, and handsome men get hit on a lot more than plain ones. And men are emotional creatures who need more than looks in a woman to be happy, and who will fall in love with a woman who makes them feel special and cared for.

Men Approach Dating Differently Than Women

So now that we've debunked some of the most common stereotypes about men, it's time to focus on how men approach dating and how their approach is different from ours. Here are the important points:

Men pursue. Single men are always on the lookout for women. They will try to find ways to talk to you or get to know you. Once you initiate things, they'll usually take the lead and ask you out, call you, or otherwise pursue you. Every guy does it a little differently, but they do it. This doesn't mean you can never ask a guy out. It means that if you've shown your interest and he isn't pursuing things with you, it's time to move on.

Men notice looks first. The first thing that interests a man is how a woman looks. If she's attractive to him physically, he'll want to take the next step. Women may be first attracted to a man's looks, but just as often she's attracted to something else about him—his personality, his accomplishments, something he does—before she finds him physically attractive. It's easy to think this makes men shallow, but it's just the way they're wired. Most men know to look beyond physical appearance, but you increase your chances of attracting a guy by looking attractive! Likewise, attractive women shouldn't assume a new man is interested in her (rather than her looks) until he proves himself over time.

Men talk about themselves. On a date, some men will talk a lot about themselves or even brag. These men don't yet understand that women don't like this! Often, though, they do this because they're nervous or because they're trying to impress you and show you what they've got going on. Just jump in the conversation. Hopefully, he'll tone it down.

Men feel sexual feelings before emotional ones. This is a key gender difference. A man can feel sexual attraction for a woman before he knows her that well, if at all. These feelings can be powerful and make a guy very interested in a woman. This is why a guy might chase a woman, sleep with her, and then disappear—the emotional feelings didn't develop. Women, on the other hand, often feel an emotional connection more quickly, before or at the same time as sexual attraction. By the time she sleeps with a guy, she's probably interested in more than sex. The important point here is to understand that a guy's initial interest in you may be physical. If you're interested in him beyond sex, it's better to avoid jumping in too soon until you know where he stands. Fortunately, many men have learned to look beyond what their dick wants and avoid getting involved with women they only feel sexual toward.

Overall, in some ways, men approach dating differently than women. But there are also a few ways men and women are the same. For example, men fear rejection just as much as we do. They find dating just as challenging as we do. Also, men may not show their feelings easily, but they have them just like we do and they don't like being insulted or criticized. Forgetting this is a fatal mistake. And they take breakups really hard. Often, we think men don't feel as much pain after a breakup because many men tend to rebound quickly; but rebounding is a sign a man isn't over a relationship and is looking for another woman to fill the hole in his life.

The Best Ways to Turn a Guy Off

When it comes to dating, each man is unique, and each has different needs and tastes. However, if you talk to enough men, you will see that there are certain things women do that many men don't like. Here they are:

Moving Too Fast

Moving too fast means you're moving faster than he's moving. Of all the mistakes you can make, this one's the biggest. Even nice guys who want a relationship were freaked out by women who moved too quickly. One guy told me that a woman he'd only seen a couple of times told him she could see him being her soul mate. Some women will drop the L word or want to move in with a guy before he's even thought about it. Women who do this don't seem to realize their date is two steps behind them! If you tend to move fast or come on too strong, step back and try to read him a little better. Let him take the lead—if he expresses interest, you can too. If he drops the L word, you're in the clear to do the same. Mistake #9 will discuss this topic in more detail.

Talking Too Much

Men often complain that some women will talk too much about themselves on a date, or they'll talk excessively to fill in conversation lulls. While sometimes this is due to self-absorption, more often it's due to nervousness. Remember: it's okay to be nervous! Talking too much only makes both of you more nervous. If you're a talker, just remember to ask him about himself, and listen as much as you talk. Overall, this is a universal complaint—men make this mistake just as much as women do.

Talking about the Ex or the Past

Everybody has an ex. We date because it didn't work out with the ex. Every time you talk about your ex, it tells a guy your ex is still important to you, which takes away from him and your date. This is a huge faux pas that both sexes are guilty of. First, get over your exes. When you date, don't talk about exes until you get to know a guy, and even then, a little goes a long way. The same goes with talking about your troubled past.

Always Expecting Him to Pay

Who pays is a controversial dating topic. Women don't always know how to approach it. Men can get pretty touchy about it—they hate feeling like they're some woman's sugar daddy or that they're being used for free meals. And let's face it: in this day and age, women are independent and can afford to pay for a meal. Here's the deal: most men enjoy paying for a date, but it annoys them when women just expect it. *Always* be appreciative of this bit of chivalry. Also, most men don't mind paying for the first couple of dates, but appreciate when a woman offers to contribute after that. Depending on his personality and finances, he may or may not let you chip in, but the fact that you offered makes him feel like he isn't being taken for granted.

Lying about Your Age or Using Old Photos Online

Online dating is full of people attempting to cover up or lie about some aspects of themselves. They try to emphasize their assets and downplay their liabilities. Men may exaggerate their height or income, and women may lie about their age or body type, either directly or by displaying photos of when they were younger or thinner.

When you date online, be honest. Use recent photos that look like you—just pick the most flattering ones. Don't lie in the hopes of casting a wider net. If you aren't proud of who you are, why should he be? Like you learned in Mistake #4, online daters get sucked into being picky. But many men will venture outside their picky criteria if they find a woman interesting or attractive. If you find a guy you like and almost meet his criteria, contact him.

> Melinda, thirty-five, has a very good figure that isn't super thin or athletic, but is attractive to most men. However, while dating on Match.com, she found that most of the men she liked were picky about body type, preferring women in the "slender" or "athletic and toned" categories rather than her "about average" category. Instead of lying about her body type, she contacted men who were a good match, regardless of what body type they wanted. She found that the majority of the men she contacted were interested in talking to her.

Coming On Too Strong

Most guys don't mind a woman who makes the first move or shows her interest, but coming on too strong makes them uncomfortable. One shy guy I spoke to said one woman he dated seemed overly eager to kiss him and wouldn't let the date end, like she wanted to "drag him back to her apartment." Women often assume that men always want sex, and some women will come on strong because they believe that's what men want. But guys don't always want to move as quickly as you think.

When you come on too strong, it's a turnoff, just like when men do it to you. And when it comes to sexy, subtle is much better than obvious when you're getting to know a guy. If you're over the top, he'll assume, right or wrong, that you're looking for sex only or that you're insecure and desperate for attention. If you're the bold type, pay attention —if you sense that a guy isn't comfortable with your overtures, back off.

Being Negative

While most women won't talk down to a date or yell at a waiter, some will make negative comments about their exes, about other people, or about their jobs or some other aspect of life. Negativity is a huge turnoff and a sign of anger and unhappiness. If you find yourself making negative comments, try to work on whatever is bugging you so it won't leak out on your dates.

Do Some Man Research

As this section has shown you, if you want to succeed with men, it helps to understand men. So how do you do this? There are many ways—but here are three of the best.

Hang Out with Men

You want to "get" men? Spend time with them. This may seem obvious, but most women spend the majority of their time around other women. They work around women, go to yoga classes filled with women, then hang out with their women friends. When you hang around men, you become familiar with them. You find out what matters to them and you learn how to talk to them.

The men you hang with can include any men: male friends, male coworkers, your dad, your brothers, or cousins. It doesn't matter if they're single or married, young or old, handsome or plain. Talk on the phone with your dad. Hang out with your brother and his buddies now and again. Go grab lunch with your male coworkers. Here are some places and activities to try:

Outdoor activities. Whether it's running, biking, hiking, ultimate Frisbee, camping, or beach volleyball, men will take part. They might even teach you to play. You can also join clubs and groups that specialize in these activities.

Sporting events. Go to a baseball game, football game, or any game. There will be two zillion men there, and you can talk to them about the rules of the game or the umpire's last call.

Bars. Sports bars, particularly during games, are filled with men. Belly up to the bar, order a drink, and ask the bartender or the guy next to you who's playing or what the score is.

Don't go to these places with the intent of meeting men to date; go simply to be around men, regardless of what type of men they are. This will lower your expectations of them and help you see them as people. You will to get to know men better, come to appreciate them more, and become used to interacting with them. Not surprisingly, the men who spend time with women and learn to appreciate them are the ones who have the most success with women. Likewise, spending time with men will give you an advantage.

Ask Men's Opinions

A good way to get to know men is to ask their opinion on something, particularly something related to dating. Not all of them will have useful or helpful opinions and you won't agree with (or even like) everything they say. Again, focus less on one man's opinion and more on the pattern of opinions you hear. If one guy says he likes lingerie, who cares? But if twenty guys say it, it's time to buy some lingerie!

When you ask men their opinions, don't judge them on their answers. You don't have to agree with them, but don't bust their chops. If you do, they'll stop talking to you and feel judged for being who they are. Remember: all information is power, whether good or bad. You aren't marrying these guys, you're getting to know them. Also, don't base your opinions of men on the small group you hang out with. Twentysomething men are different than men in their forties. Blue-collar men are different from men in white-collar jobs. Southern men are different than New Yorkers. White men are different than black men. Men who come from rough or abusive upbringings differ from men raised in healthy families. All in all, they're still men—but they will have unique characteristics.

Read Dating Advice Written for Men

While reading is no substitute for personal experience, you can learn *a lot* about men by reading dating advice written for men. Just be prepared for the fact that you won't like or agree with everything you read. Some of it will anger or even repulse you. But remember—they're just guys with opinions, and you can learn just as much from the ones you don't agree with as you can from the ones you do.

For example, one dating expert warns men that if women ask them what they do for a living, it's because the women are trying to assess how much money they make. This expert feels that women care most about how much money a guy makes. This irritates me—when I ask a guy what he does, it's to make conversation! You can tell a lot about what makes a guy tick by what he does for a living. But reading this guy's advice helped me understand that 1) men are concerned about gold diggers and about spending too much on women and getting nothing in return, and 2) this guy's acidic advice came from his own negative experiences.

Here's a list of books or websites to check out:

John Gray's _Men Are from Mars, Women Are from Venus_ series. These books are written for both sexes, but it's nice to get a man's point of view. There's the original book as well as several others, including one on dating. Not everyone agrees with Gray (including me at times), but he is more insightful than most on male-female differences and is definitely worth reading.

Neil Strauss's _The Game._ A _Rolling Stone_ reporter, Strauss joined a group of pickup artists and became one himself, learning about women, men, and himself on the way. This book is not only an interesting read, it will show you the lengths men will go to attract women.

Askmen.com. This website for men covers everything from sports, cars, and finances to movies, clothes, and wine. It has a large section on sex and dating with advice on many topics. The advice here can range from pretty good to pretty lame, but it will give you a good idea of the types of things men struggle with.

There are also many other books written by men for men, especially books on how pick up, seduce, or otherwise get women into bed. Even if you find these books repulsive, you will learn a lot about the sorts of things men struggle with or worry about. Hopefully you'll see that dating is no easier for them than it is for you.

Hopefully this section will improve your dating success by helping you to understand men better and see things from their point of view. Whether it's men, kids, your parents, your boss, or the guy who makes your latte, the better you are at seeing things from others' point of view, the better you'll get along with them. When we judge others, often it's because we've never stood in their shoes. We don't understand them. The same is true with men and dating. You will never get to be a man, but if you work at understanding men better, you'll find yourself enjoying dating and relationships more.

Mistake #6

You Think You Need to Be a Supermodel

> "There are no ugly women, only lazy ones."
>
> HELENA RUBENSTEIN

Like it or not, looks are important. They're important in life, and they're important in dating. How you look is the first thing guys see, and your attractiveness factor is the first criterion guys evaluate you on. And the more attractive you are, the better chance you have of attracting the man you want.

However, that being said, most women misunderstand what really attracts men, and why. On top of that, most women are way too hard on themselves about their looks. All of this only makes dating more difficult. How can you really date successfully if you don't know what makes a woman attractive or you're always worried about being pretty enough? Feeling good about yourself and your attractiveness is essential to dating. So this entire section is devoted to showing you that Mistake #6 is counterproductive and totally unnecessary.

Beauty versus Attractiveness

Beauty and attractiveness are *not* the same thing. Beauty, or what many would call "outer beauty," is what your DNA handed you. It is strictly physical, and includes your body shape and proportion and your facial features. There isn't a lot you can do to change these things, and some women are just more naturally beautiful than others.

Attractiveness, on the other hand, is a broader term—it's your ability to attract people, including men. This is done through physical appearance, but also through what comes from inside of you. Beauty is part of attractiveness, but attractiveness is much more than beauty. Attractiveness is about what you do with what you have, and who you are as a person. It's about how you take care of yourself, the effort you put in, how you feel about yourself, and how you relate to others. Attractiveness is reflected in your hairstyle, clothes, personality, self-confidence, and your attitude toward life. Attractiveness certainly comes through when you start talking to a man, but he can also see it before he ever talks to you. The good thing about attractiveness is that you have a lot of control over how much of it you've got. The other good thing about it is that if you do it right, people will think you're beautiful!

The reason it's especially important to understand the difference between beauty and attractiveness is that most people think attractiveness is just about beauty. Likewise, women think they need beauty to attract a man, but what they really need is attractiveness. True, beauty will always attract men; but it won't keep them around. Attractiveness will get them—and keep them.

Sometimes it can be difficult to differentiate between what is beautiful and what is attractive. Check out these examples of women whose beauty does not prevent them from being unattractive at times.

My friend Susan is very pretty and often gets hit on when we're out together. She enjoys traveling the world, but when she travels alone she prefers to avoid attracting men. To deal with unwanted male attention, particularly in countries where men are bold, she knows just what to do. She pulls her hair up and hides it under a big hat or a handkerchief, wears loose-fitting, boring clothes that cover her, and doesn't wear makeup. Nobody bothers her.

On a past season of *The Bachelor*, one contestant had the kind of looks that made men's heads turn and was an early favorite of the Bachelor. He invited her to go out on a fancy date, something not all the girls got to do. But this woman rarely had anything of substance to say, and she gave off a negative energy that turned many of the girls against her. While the Bachelor admitted that he liked how she looked, he quickly lost interest in her and she was eliminated from the show.

These examples illustrate the difference between beauty and attractiveness. Each of these women was pretty, even beautiful, but had managed to make herself much less attractive through her hairstyle, clothing, or behavior.

So, knowing that a woman's attractiveness is much more than her outer beauty, how does that translate to attracting men?

The Threshold Effect

If you want to understand how a man evaluates a woman's attractiveness, including before he ever talks to her, you have to understand the Threshold Effect. The Threshold Effect essentially means that for you to be interested in someone, that someone needs to be above a certain threshold when it comes to attractiveness. The figure below illustrates how we generally evaluate a guy's attractiveness:

1	5	10
Not at all attractive	Not so cute	Decent looking	Cute	Very cute	Hot as hell

When you check out men, you may put them somewhere along this one-to-ten scale. Even if you don't assign an actual number, you use this general system when you evaluate guys. The more attractive they are to you, the further to the right they'll be.

However, we all have a certain cutoff on this scale, where guys below the cutoff aren't attractive to us, but guys above the cutoff are. You may only be interested in men who are, roughly, a six or higher. In that case, six is your threshold. This way of thinking about attractiveness is shown in the figure below:

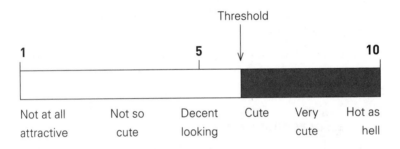

Generally speaking, if six is your threshold, you'll go out with guys above a six, but not with guys below six. If he's a great guy and you like him, you don't care much if he's a six, an eight, or a ten, as long as he's at least a six. And when you check men out, you will automatically rule out ones, threes, and fives. This doesn't mean they're bad guys; they may even be cute. But they aren't attractive enough to you. And what's cool is that when you fall for a great guy who's a six, he will probably start to look more like a nine to you!

The Threshold Effect isn't just about how good looking a guy is. Many people think they're using a one-to-ten scale to describe beauty, but more often they're describing attractiveness without even knowing it. When we first check a guy out, beauty plays a bigger role in our interest, but this can change once we talk to him. This is why a five can turn into a seven once you get to know him and see how great he is, and why a nine can plummet to a five once you find out he's a big jerk.

Also, the Threshold Effect is personal—it's about how attractive a guy is to *you*. It's subjective, based on your personal tastes and feelings. A guy who's a seven to you may only be a four to your friend.

The Threshold Effect works for men too. While it's common for men to check out women and rate them on a one-to-ten scale, most make their dating decisions based on the Threshold Effect. Most men have a cutoff, and any woman above that threshold is fair game. A woman's beauty will play into a guy's choice, but most men evaluate attractiveness too, especially after he starts talking to her. A woman who started out as a five may jump to a seven once he sees how cool she is. And where a woman falls on this spectrum, and whether or not she is above his threshold, is somewhat subjective for men, like it is with women. Sure, very pretty women are more likely to be above the average guy's threshold. But an attractive woman may be one guy's five and another guy's eight.

So how does all of this apply to your dating life? First, it means that you only need to be above the threshold of the men you like. You don't have to look like a model, or anything close to one. If a man falls for you, he'll think you're beautiful anyway. This is important because most women put too much emphasis on beauty and not enough on attractiveness when it comes to dating.

Second, men's thresholds aren't nearly as high as you think. Most are around six. And because thresholds are individual, you may be very attractive and still fall below a man's threshold. Finally, finding someone who is above our threshold is only the first step in a multistep process. A lot of people will be above our threshold; but ultimately, chemistry and compatibility determine how far the relationship goes.

Do You Sell Yourself Short?

So now you know the importance of not confusing beauty with attractiveness. Next, you'll learn the other half of the problem when it comes to your looks: women are too hard on themselves about their beauty. More importantly, women put too much emphasis on beauty and not enough emphasis on attractiveness, which makes dating a lot harder than it needs to be. Don't worry—anyone can make this dating mistake, *including men*. Attractiveness, i.e., your ability to attract others through your physical appearance as well as who you are inside, is much more important than outer beauty for successful dating.

This section discusses some ways women sell themselves short in this area, and how it negatively affects their dating lives.

You Think Beauty Is More Important Than Attractiveness

Of the many ways women sell themselves short, this is the most common, and the most troublesome. Women are hard on themselves, especially about their looks. Beauty and fashion are multibillion dollar industries; I often joke that if these industries were to suddenly shut down, the economy of the western world would probably collapse. There's nothing wrong with beauty or fashion, of course. Wanting to look good is natural; it's in our genes. Women across the planet have dressed their bodies, faces, and hair since the dawn of time. The problem is that our society has become too beauty-oriented and has forgotten that outer beauty isn't enough to make a person worthwhile.

I recently watched a TV show that showed paparazzi photos of celebrity women hanging out in their spare time. They wore no makeup and their hair wasn't done—they didn't look glamorous, but most of them looked pretty good. Yet the show criticized every one of them for not looking "beautiful" enough. Tabloid magazines find pictures of female celebrities with cellulite, weight gain, or any other flaw. With such trash in our faces all the time, it's no wonder we begin to think outer beauty is all that matters!

Another reason women think beauty is more important than attractiveness is that we listen to the comments men make about women. Some guys will gawk at beauties, and then make a critical comment about a woman who isn't beautiful. We then automatically think we need to be beautiful to get a guy. But this isn't true for several reasons:

Guys are attracted to appearance first. Because men are often attracted first to a woman's looks, we assume they're picky about looks. Women care about men's looks too, but they aren't always the thing that attracts us first. But just because a guy enjoys looking at beauty doesn't mean that's all that matters to him. And let's be honest: we all check out people and critique their appearance, whether out loud or to ourselves.

Men want someone they connect with. Just like outer beauty isn't enough to make a person worthwhile, it isn't enough to keep a man's interest. Men only looking for a conquest, a trophy, or an ego boost will focus on looks only. But men looking for someone to spend time with want a woman they like, not just one who looks good.

Men don't differentiate beauty and attractiveness. For many men, if they feel attracted to a woman, then she is beautiful, even if she isn't actually beautiful. Remember, the Threshold Effect is individual; every man has different tastes. A girl who's nice looking to one guy may be hot to another. Likewise, if a guy isn't attracted to a woman, he will rarely think she's beautiful, even if she is.

Men aren't nearly as finicky about looks as women are. A lot of the reason we might think men are picky about beauty is because *we* are. When it comes to beauty, women are much tougher judges than men.

Back in college, a girlfriend and I went out to a bar. We got there early and wound up catching a contest where young women would dance and strip down to bathing suits. All of the women were pretty and had nice bodies. When I told my friend who my favorite was, my friend looked at the one I'd chosen and said, "She has stretch marks." If you looked very closely, you could see pale stretch marks on this woman's hips.

Because we were so close to the contestants, I too had noticed the stretch marks, but they did not detract from her beauty. I was shocked at my friend's pettiness. I guarantee you that 98 percent of the men there did not care about, or even notice, that woman's tiny flaw. Only a woman would be that critical.

Because we're such tough critics of ourselves, we can be tough critics of other women as well. Likewise, we assume men want perfection in us because we want it in ourselves. But men don't want perfection—they want someone they find attractive. If men were that picky about outer beauty, most of us would be single forever and the hot chicks would have harems of men feeding them grapes day and night. Many women think they aren't attractive enough to men because they don't meet whatever beauty standard they hold for themselves.

But what about those of you who are beautiful and used to men's attention? Thinking beauty is more important than attractiveness can be a trap for you too. Consider the questions below:

- Have you always been told that you're beautiful?
- Do you believe that your looks are your best asset?
- Do you spend more time and money on looking good than other women you know?
- Have you had cosmetic surgery?
- Do you attract of lot of men who then become disinterested or turn into total jerks?
- Do you fear getting older, wondering if you won't find a good man because you're not young anymore?

Regardless of how beautiful you are, if you answered yes to even one of these questions, you are at risk for thinking beauty is more important than attractiveness. If you answered yes to more than one of the questions, you're at high risk.

Outer beauty can be a curse. It can make beautiful women believe that their looks are the only thing that makes them worthwhile. It can attract men who care only about looks. If you're beautiful, be careful. Don't fall into the trap of thinking outer beauty is more important than attractiveness and who you are as a person. You will attract lots of men, but they won't always be the best men, so it's important to be very cautious and date only quality men who like you for who you are. Remember: men are attracted to appearance first. The more physically attractive you are, the more wrong men you'll attract.

Here's an example of this: Taryn and I worked once together in the same office. Taryn was smokin' hot, and a lot of guys we worked with were interested in her. But when I looked at who these guys were, I wasn't impressed. One of them cheated on his girlfriend, who worked at our office, with another woman who worked there. Another was a cocky jerk. A third one smoked weed constantly and had the intellect of a brick. They had nothing in common with her and were only interested in her for her looks. Fortunately, she knew that beauty wasn't enough. She ignored these guys and dated a guy who liked her for who she was. Today, they're still together and have two kids.

Remember the pretty woman from *The Bachelor*, who quickly lost the Bachelor's interest because she was beautiful but not attractive in other ways? When he rejected her, she got angry. She was used to being admired by men and couldn't believe he rejected her. She couldn't see that they had nothing in common and that he wasn't attracted beyond the physical. She couldn't see that beauty isn't enough. Even if she'd been a more attractive person in other ways, it's still no guarantee he would have liked her. No matter how beautiful a woman is, not every man will find her attractive. Beauty can create chemistry, but it cannot create compatibility—and you must have both to make it work with a guy.

Thinking beauty is more important than attractiveness is a no-win gig, regardless of how much outer beauty you've got going. Don't sell yourself short in this way. Later in this section you'll learn the elements of attractiveness.

You Aren't as Attractive as You Could Be

While putting too much stock in your looks is a mistake, so is not putting enough stock in them. Physical attractiveness is still key to attracting men; it's the first thing they see about you and it makes a strong first impression. Fortunately, attractiveness, including physical attractiveness, is something any woman can achieve. And the more attractive you are, the more likely you are to attract the men you like. Yet, despite this, many women aren't as attractive as they could be. Here are some examples of how women sell themselves short in this way:

Not making an effort to look good. One of men's greatest complaints about marriage is that their wives let themselves go physically. You might argue with that and say that men are shallow, but everyone wants an attractive partner. The real issue with most of these men isn't that their wives get older or put on a few pounds; it's that they stop trying. A lack of effort will annoy a husband who loves you, but in dating it will cause a guy to not even look your way. The magic word here is *effort*: you can tell the difference between a woman who tries and one who doesn't. You can be beautiful or plain, a corporate suit type or a jeans-and-tees girl, young or old—if you put effort into how you look, people will recognize it and find you more attractive.

Not taking care of your health. Poor health habits will take a big toll on your looks. They also influence how you feel on a day-to-day basis, which also affects your looks. Taking care of your health includes eating well, exercising, and managing stress in your life. Stress by itself will ruin your health and make you look and feel awful.

Being unhappy or negative about life. Unhappiness and negativity are very unattractive. They show in your body language and in how you express yourself. You'll get less attention and fewer second dates because men fear that your unhappiness will bring them down.

Lacking goals or direction in life. Have you ever met a woman who was really pretty but had no life? Maybe she had no job or goals, and just waited for a man to come into her life and give her something to do. Men like women with goals and hobbies; it's less pressure on them.

Lacking confidence in who you are. A lack of confidence isn't attractive. Not all of us are confident in every area and we all have our insecurities. But it's hard to be attracted to someone who lacks confidence in too many areas and who doesn't believe in herself.

You don't have to spend a lot of time or money to be attractive. But making an effort to be attractive pays off, just like making an effort pays off in other areas of life.

You Obsess about Your Age

When it comes to attracting men, women have always been concerned about their age. Long ago, thirty was the age single women would freak out about—if you weren't married by thirty, then hell, there must be something wrong you! Although some women still fear turning thirty, times have changed and women have pushed back their "worry age." Some of this worry has to do with fertility and the desire to have kids, which makes sense. But most of it has to do with believing that as you age, you won't be attractive to men anymore.

A lot of the age issue is similar to the beauty issue—in the same way women believe they aren't attractive if they aren't beautiful, they believe they aren't attractive if they aren't twenty-one. Popular culture, which is very youth oriented, only reinforces this unhealthy belief. Movies tend to pair older men with much younger women. And men don't help—when you date online and see men who only want women younger than themselves, it makes you wonder. And how many of you have been hit on by men who are old enough to be your father?

Whether you're thirty, forty, or fifty, if you think beauty is more important than attractiveness, you'll worry about your age because outer beauty does fade a little with age. You're definitely selling yourself short! The truth is, you don't need to obsess about your age when you date, for several reasons. First, while many men may find younger women attractive, most recognize that their attraction is physical and don't date them because they feel they have nothing in common with them. There are some men who chase young women for their own ego gratification—these men are insecure and have something to prove, so why would you want to date them anyway?

Second, many men find older women attractive. If she's attractive to him, he doesn't care how old she is. But while older men will hit on younger women, younger men rarely hit on older women because they feel too intimidated. They assume older women prefer an older, more sophisticated man. Many times, they're right—most women don't give younger men the time of day.

Finally, older women/younger men relationships have become more prevalent in recent years. There are many reasons for this, but men tell me that one of them is that older women have certain qualities they like. For example:

Security with one's self. Older women are more comfortable with who they are. Life experience gives them this, and people who are comfortable with themselves are often better company.

Less drama. If there's one thing men hate, it's drama. And let's face it: many younger people are more easily upset, more hormone-driven, and less experienced at dealing with the ups and downs of everyday life.

More independence. As they age, women learn to take care of themselves instead of hoping a man will take care of them. This is true financially as well as emotionally. Men often feel pressured by the expectation that women need a lot of taking care of. Older women are more likely to have well-paying jobs, satisfying careers, and to enjoy personal space. And some men prefer women over the age of forty because they're less likely to pressure them about getting married or having kids.

More assertiveness. Older women know what they want and are willing to ask for it. One of men's biggest frustrations with women is that they expect men to read their minds and figure out what they want. Older women have learned to just ask.

Better sex. Older women are more experienced and more likely to ask for what they want in bed. This makes for better sex for both parties. Men strongly prefer women who love sex and state what they want in bed.

However, there are two things men complain about with a few of the older women they've dated. One is bitterness; some men, especially if they're over forty, complain that women in that age bracket are bitter about men, about their divorces, about the dating scene. As discussed in Mistake #2, a bad attitude is a *huge* turnoff. This is one reason why some older men chase much younger women—younger women are less likely to be bitter.

The second thing is lack of attractiveness. For many, looking good doesn't take much effort when you're young. But when you get older, you have to put some effort into it. If you make the effort and develop the other areas of attractiveness, you will have no trouble attracting men at any age.

Beauty may fade a little with age, but many of the other elements of attractiveness actually improve. Women become more confident, more successful, and more comfortable with themselves as they get older. So, as you can see, selling yourself short by worrying about your age is unnecessary. Attractiveness is ageless, if you're willing to make the effort.

How to Be a Man Magnet

Okay, so I've talked about how important attractiveness is and how women sell themselves short. Now, let's get to the practical stuff—the factors that make up attractiveness:

Looks

As you know, physical attractiveness is important to attracting men. It's the first thing they see, and it's how they develop their initial interest in a woman. Looks aren't enough to keep a man's attention or to make a relationship work, but they definitely increase your attractiveness factor.

You can't do much about what you were born with, but you can do a lot to increase your physical attractiveness with some effort. Effort is about what you do with what you have, through hair and wardrobe, fitness, and good health. Looking good isn't about following some formula. It isn't about big boobs or tight skirts or high heels. Sure, men like these things; but looking good is about more than that.

I did get one good thing out of watching that silly show about celebrity women seen without makeup: I saw that beautiful celebrity women look normal, even unrecognizable, when you take them out of their red carpet get-up. This shows us that effort, not perfection, is most important, even for celebrities.

Although there are many sources where you can get advice on looking good, here are a few items to consider. Each of these things will attract men regardless of your beauty or your age, and they don't require you to change who you are as a person.

- **Get a great hairstyle.** Because men typically keep their hair short, a woman's hair is often the first thing that attracts them. A great hairstyle can make an average woman look amazing. A bad hairstyle will do the opposite. Hire an expert to help if necessary, but make sure you choose a style that works with your face, your hair type, and your personality.
- **Go easy on the makeup.** I've heard one or two men complain about women who don't wear enough makeup, but I've heard countless men complain about women who wear too much. You want men to notice you, not your makeup.

- **Get a great wardrobe.** A clothing makeover can absolutely transform a woman who looks frumpy and unattractive to one who looks amazing, even if you change nothing else about her. Find clothing that fits your body as well as your personal style. Also, avoid wearing old, outdated clothing—you don't have to follow trends, but lagging behind them is unattractive. A man may not notice specific clothing items, but he will definitely notice what a good outfit does for you.
- **Stay in shape.** While you don't need to be super thin or super fit, keeping a good figure is important in physical attractiveness. Although some men want thin women, many men are happy with average-sized or curvy figures if they look feminine, dress well, and take good care of themselves.

Friendliness

If you want to get a guy's attention, smile and appear friendly. Open up your body language: uncross your arms, make eye contact, and turn your body toward him. By itself, smiling has an almost magical effect on people that is mostly unconscious. People will respond to a smile before they even realize what they're doing, even if the smile wasn't intended for them. When I smile about something I'm thinking about, I find that men talk to me a lot more.

Friendly, open people are not only pleasant to be around, but they're also perceived as more attractive. Research has shown that, given equivalent levels of attractiveness, men rate women who have friendly or open body language as more attractive than women who don't. In the dating world, friendly women get more attention from men. They're more approachable and more attractive.

It makes sense. Friendly, open people are usually happy people, and happy people are a pleasure to be around. They make others feel good. If you're genuinely friendly and open, men will feel good around you and be more attracted to you.

Confidence

When you ask people, male or female, what they find attractive in the opposite sex, they'll often say confidence. Confidence is an extremely attractive quality and plays a huge role in your attractiveness factor. Confidence is believing in yourself; you may not know everything or know how to handle a given situation, but you believe in your ability to handle whatever comes your way and you try your best. Imagine how helpful this quality is when you date! If you walk into a dating situation knowing that you can handle yourself, you're in good shape. And confidence puts other people at ease, which also helps during dating.

Most people aren't hugely confident. But a reasonable amount of confidence goes a long way. However, don't confuse confidence with arrogance. Arrogance is being full of yourself, feeling you're always right, and believing your accomplishments or abilities make you better than other people. People often believe arrogance is excessive confidence, but it's really a lack of confidence. Arrogant people are insecure, and often repel others. Truly confident people feel good about themselves and attract others to them.

Success

Male or female, successful people are attractive because they've shown that they're willing to work hard and get what they want out of life. Because achieving success isn't easy, a successful person stands out. And success isn't just about money—it's about having goals in life, and working diligently toward them without giving up. Successful women are more common these days: women go to college, comprise more than 50 percent of medical school students, work in powerful professions, run their own businesses, and compete at the elite level in sports.

Some professional women complain that men are threatened by successful women. Any man who's threatened by a woman's success is insecure about himself and his own lack of success in life. It's that simple. However, while some men are crybabies about women's success, most men aren't. Women who consistently have this problem may find that it isn't the men, it's them. Like some accomplished men, some successful women are too aggressive, arrogant, or competitive. These women try to prove how smart and powerful they are, that they can compete in a man's world. This may work in business, but it fails in relationships. Men like successful women, not women who need to prove they're better than men.

> Michelle is Harvard-educated, well-read, and very bright. She's held powerful positions in major law firms and is very successful. However, the men she dates are never smart enough for her. She has extremely strong opinions about many things, and if a man says something she disagrees with, she will argue until she feels she wins the argument. She then tells her friends how stupid or wrong he is. Despite being very pretty, Michelle turns men off and rarely dates.

No man wants to be looked down on. I have a PhD and I'm a published author, and most of the men I meet aren't intimidated—they're impressed. While I'm proud of my accomplishments, they don't define who I am or make me better than anyone else.

Being Comfortable With Yourself

Being comfortable with yourself is a bit like self-confidence, except it focuses less on believing in yourself and your ability to handle things and focuses more on liking yourself. Liking who you are and being comfortable in your own skin comes from knowing yourself and accepting yourself. When you like yourself, others like you—and that includes men.

A woman who's comfortable with herself is comfortable with her assets and her flaws, both physically and otherwise. Women who aren't comfortable with themselves tend to:

- Criticize other women
- Have bad attitudes about men
- Get upset over small things or take everything personally
- Resent people who are successful or confident in themselves
- Have a difficult time accepting a compliment

People who like themselves are not only more attractive, they're also more pleasant to be around. You'll find that when you become more comfortable with yourself, you'll be more accepting of others as well.

Men Are Insecure Too (Even the Hot Ones)

I've spent quite a while talking about the ways women are hard on themselves and how they sell themselves short in terms of their attractiveness to men. But if it makes you feel any better, men are insecure about their attractiveness too.

In the physical attractiveness department, two of the biggest things men worry about are penis size and hair loss. They also worry about their weight, their love handles, and their "bird legs." They worry that they aren't big enough, tall enough, muscular enough, and that they can't get a six pack no matter how hard they try. They aren't as perfectionist as women are, but guys want to look good too. They also worry that if they don't look good they won't attract as many women.

And it isn't just the average-looking guys who say these things. Really good-looking men are just as insecure. Like women, they'll zero in on some area of weakness in themselves. One very handsome, intelligent man I spoke to worried about an extra ten pounds around his middle. Another very good-looking, very tall twenty-eight-year-old with an amazing body felt insecure about his height. The hot guys get rejected too, and they too struggle with dating and finding the right woman.

Men are also concerned about aging. They worry about losing their youthful bodies and their athletic abilities. And although men have the ability to reproduce when they're older, that isn't what they want. They have biological clocks too—what man wants to be so much older than his kid that he can't even relate to him? What man hopes he'll be too old and out of shape to play baseball with his son? There isn't a man in the world who wishes for that.

Men worry about their ability to please a woman in bed. They worry about being successful enough or having enough cash to attract a woman. Men want to attract women, and they notice when women flock to guys with nice cars or gorgeous bodies. Women may think they need to be Gisele Bündchen, but often, men wish they were Tom Brady.

Overall, we all want the same thing: to attract a good partner. You can, as long as you focus on what's most important—being attractive from the inside out.

Mistake #7

You Let Him
Choose You

> **"Women not only control the game and make the rules, they own the scoreboard."**
>
> *THE DEFINITIVE BOOK OF BODY LANGUAGE*

Years ago, I was working out at my gym, and could feel a guy looking at me. I turned to look at him—just then, he quickly looked away. I'd seen him before and he was cute. Seriously cute. The next time I saw him, he looked at me again and then made eye contact with me. Eventually, he smiled at me. But he did not come talk to me! And I didn't feel comfortable talking to him—the weight room is not the place for chatting it up, and I'm a bit shy. This wasn't the first time this had happened to me. I was interested in this guy, he seemed interested in me, and I didn't want to miss yet another opportunity. I didn't know what to do, so I posted on a public online forum, where I described my situation and told the guys I wanted their advice. The guys responded—lots of them. And the message from all of them was basically the same:

- They're afraid of rejection.
- They're afraid of bothering women who don't want to be bothered.
- They don't want to be "That Guy"—that chumpy dude who hits on uninterested women and gets blown off.
- They need a signal of some sort, like a smile or a hello. Once they get that signal, they'll take over from there.

Each of these guys could relate to my predicament. They'd all been there. And not one guy said "we prefer to make the first move" or "we'll approach if we're truly interested." Interestingly, I did get one response from a female who told me that if my guy "doesn't have the balls" to talk to me, then he isn't worth bothering with, and then added that he's probably not that interested in me. Her response was the exact opposite of the guys' responses! And, as you will see, she didn't have a clue. In the end, did I get a date with Mr. Cutie? Hell no! Why? Because I made it too hard for him.

Since that experience, I've done extensive research on how to meet or break the ice with a guy who interests you. My situation took place at the gym, but the challenge is the same for meeting pretty much anywhere else, whether it's the grocery store, the local beer joint, or your girlfriend's cocktail party. I've interviewed countless men, and they tell me the same thing as the men who e-mailed me. Sure, we've all met those guys who are bold: the loud guy at the sports bar who says you're hot, the guy who asks you out when you've only known him fifteen seconds, or the wannabe player who hits on tons of women, hoping that one will say yes. But those guys are the exception, and they're never the guys we're interested in!

The truth is, *initiating contact with someone who interests you is probably the most difficult and challenging task of dating, for men or women.* Because it's so hard, we'll often admire someone from afar rather than take a risk. More often, we girls sit back and expect the guys to take the initiative and make a move. And by doing that, we get offers from the wrong guys, or no guys at all, and then we complain about how hard it is to meet good guys. This, ladies, is Mistake #7: you let men do the choosing.

Why Women Are Supposed to Initiate

Despite what you may have heard, women are supposed to initiate things with men, not the other way around. One reason that you should initiate is that women tend to overestimate men's courage. Yes, men have balls. They'll break their bones riding motorcycles, risk all their savings to start a company, or humiliate themselves publicly like the guys on *Jackass*. But when it comes to women, most guys are terrified.

Guys hate to be rejected by women. Guys will check out women they like but then never talk to them, concoct pickup lines or other elaborate methods to approach women, or try to meet women at bars, where a few drinks will quell their fears. If you read any men's guide on picking up women, and there are LOTS of them, you'll see that making contact with women is their greatest challenge, and that it took the authors themselves many years to overcome their fears of approaching women.

Most women don't realize how hard this is for men. After all, guys do crazy things in movies to get women to notice them, right? Yes, but movies are fantasies, which is why we love them! What guy doesn't wish he had the stones to sing "You've Lost That Loving Feeling" to a beautiful woman in a bar, like Maverick did in *Top Gun*? But men do pursue us, call us, and ask us out, right? Yes, *but only when they feel they have a good chance of success*. In general, men will make a move if they have at least a 75 percent chance that she will want to talk to him, give him her phone number, or say yes to a date. Walking up to a woman who hasn't given the green light through eye contact, smiling, or some other signal has closer to a 10 percent chance of success. Those odds are enough for some guys, but not most.

This fear is a good thing. If men were that bold, you would be constantly hit on by men who don't interest you, which would suck. This is why women are supposed to initiate things—to let men know it's okay to approach or pursue. You have the upper hand in this area—use it! By initiating, you choose the men who interest you and give them the green light instead of letting them choose you and getting annoyed when they aren't the men you like. Here's a good example where a man made his move after a woman initiated things:

Hanna and Joseph both took a finance class. Hanna noticed Joseph looking at her and making eye contact, but he did not talk to her. One day, they were getting coffee at the same time, and Hanna started talking to Joseph. They talked for a while, and Joseph asked Hanna out. Later, Joseph told Hanna that he'd been attracted to her from the start, but didn't feel comfortable initiating things with her. He said he didn't like hitting on women and preferred when they broke the ice first.

So, is Joseph a guy with no balls, or is he a cautious guy who wants to make sure he's welcome before making a move? Men are vulnerable too—they want to feel valued and wanted, just like we do. Once you see this truth, you will have more compassion and MUCH greater success with men.

Another reason you should feel comfortable making the first move? Letting men do the initiating is not the way things actually happen in the real world. Not only should women initiate things with men, women often *do* initiate things, although they may not realize it. Behavioral research with both humans and animals has shown that it's typically females, not males, who initiate courtship. In many animal species, females initiate mating rituals by emitting pheromones or giving some other signal. Human mating rituals are more complex, but it's basically the same idea: women indicate their interest to males through a series of signals. When men approach women or ask them out, it's usually after they get signals that a woman is interested. These signals come from body language. Many times, women's body language, and men's ability to read it, is entirely unconscious. Researchers have actually filmed men and women interacting at a party or bar and found that women display of series of "courting signals" to men.

Here's the typical scenario:

A man finds a woman attractive and checks her out. She sees him looking, they make eye contact, and then she looks away. He looks a second time; she looks over and sees him looking again. This time she makes longer eye contact with him, and smiles. Then, he walks over to her.

In this situation, you may believe the man initiated things, but he really didn't. He checked out the woman, but it was her looking for the second time, making solid eye contact, and smiling that gave him "permission" to talk to her. She called the shots, not him.

Overall, men want to meet women, but they don't want to be the guy who approaches women who aren't interested. If women assume men are bolder than they are and wait for men to do all the work, nothing happens. This puts both sexes in a stalemate situation, where nobody gets what they really want. Most men are willing to do their part and come talk to you or ask you out, so you need to do your part and make it easy for them to do so! They won't make a move until they get a sign, so you better figure out how to send that sign!

So What Is Initiating?

Initiating is giving a guy a sign that you're open to his advances. This can be as simple as making eye contact with him, starting a conversation with him, or, in some circumstances, giving him your number. It's showing a guy that he can talk to you, call you, or ask you out, without the risk that he's bothering you when you don't want to be bothered. Initiating is not the same as hitting on a man or coming on to a man. It is not aggressive or sexual. Although some guys need pretty obvious hints, for most men it only takes one small indication of interest and he'll take it from there.

The Basics of Initiating

In order to initiate with men, you will need to understand basic courtship behaviors. These include body language, eye contact, and conversation.

Despite humans having advanced language skills, 80 percent of what we communicate is nonverbal. When you "get a sense" or "have a feeling" that a guy is interested, you're often unconsciously reading his body language. Body language becomes even more powerful when you're able to recognize it consciously, and it will help you spot guys who are interested in you as well as let them see your interest in them, both of which are important in initiating. A potentially interested guy will show these signs:

Looking. He'll look right at you, often more than once, or he'll look at you "on the sly" and turn away just as you catch him looking. The longer and more often he looks, the more interested he is.

Interested facial expression. He may smile (with his eyes, not just his lips), nod, or even tilt his head slightly. More subtle signs include raising his eyebrows (even briefly) and pupil dilation.

Proximity. He may walk by you, place himself near you, or seem to be where you are more than what you'd expect by chance. If he saw you at a particular place, he might suddenly show up there more often.

Preening behaviors. He may brush lint off his shirt, adjust his tie, or run his hand through his hair. He's unconsciously trying to look good for you.

Standing tall. He'll often stand up straighter, push his chest out, or stand with his legs apart, as if to look more masculine.

Open body language. If talking with him, he'll face you (although not necessarily completely), his feet may point toward you, and he'll have his arms at his sides or otherwise not blocking his body.

You can use these same signs to detect when a man is likely *not* interested. For example, an uninterested man will typically:

- Not look at you, or look only briefly
- Show "closed" body language such as body, legs, or feet turned away from you (as if looking to leave), or arms crossed in front of him
- Display a flat or bored expression, or give you a polite "lips only" smile

Like body language, eye contact is also a form of non-verbal communication, but it's so powerful that it deserves its own category. If you want to learn to read a man, look at his eyes. Eye contact is probably the most profound way that people telegraph their emotions, including their attraction. Eye contact is so powerful that people will avoid it in most situations. Ever been in an elevator? People won't make eye contact because they're strangers trapped in a small space together—it's too uncomfortable.

Here are different types of eye contact, and what they mean:

Type	How long it lasts	What it means
Brief	A split second	"You exist"
		"I see you"
Longer	1–2 seconds	"You're attractive"
		"I could be interested"
		"I recognize you"
Extended	3 or more seconds	"You're quite attractive"
		"I'm definitely interested"
		"You affect me"

Brief eye contact is for the average person. It's an acknowledgement of that person. Anything longer than a split second is uncomfortable, and therefore meaningful. With men, brief eye contact is a sign he isn't interested.

Longer eye contact is a little more interesting. It often signifies potential interest or recognition of an attractive person. We look longer at what we find attractive or interesting—this is true for all people, even infants. Longer eye contact is also used when people recognize one another, as with acquaintances or colleagues, in which case the eye contact is often followed by a nod or hello.

Longer eye contact from a man means he's checking you out, and may be interested.

Extended eye contact is the good stuff. It goes beyond our comfort zone, and can be powerful and highly telling. If a man you like makes eye contact with you for this long, especially if he initiates it, pay attention because it usually indicates significant levels of interest or attraction.

Overall, if you want to know if a guy's interested, look for the following:

Number of occurrences. Making eye contact with you more than one time is a sure sign of interest. If he isn't interested, he will only look once (probably briefly) or avoid eye contact altogether.

Length. Longer eye contact means greater interest. It's also a sign of boldness or confidence. Briefer or breaking of eye contact may mean less interest, but can also be a sign of shyness or intimidation.

Who initiates. If he initiates eye contact and holds it until you break it first, that's a definite sign of interest. However, extended eye contact is a good sign no matter who initiates it.

The expression in his eyes. If his eyes appear to gleam, light up, or "soften," those are good signs. Eyes that appear intense, serious, or flat are harder to read, and you'll have to rely on the above signs to determine if he's interested.

Eye contact, like other forms of body language, isn't usually done consciously. Guys don't say, "Hey, that woman is hot, I think I'll look into her eyes for two-plus seconds and see what she does." It's instinct, which is part of the reason why it's so powerful, and so telling. Not only does eye contact indicate interest, it also increases interest. Studies have shown that when two people were told to look at the other person in the eyes while they spoke, their opinions of each other went up significantly. Keep that in mind when you check a guy out.

Finally, while only 20 percent of what we communicate is verbal, that 20 percent is key if you want to close the deal with a man you're interested in. Once you've broken the sound barrier and started talking to a guy, if he's interested he will:

Want to talk. He'll find something to say. Often, he'll keep talking with you as long as he can. Men who aren't interested will avoid talking to you or if they talk, they'll seem preoccupied and will keep it brief.

Listen. He'll pay attention and be interested in what you have to say. If you run into him more than once, he'll recall your name, ask you about your physics class, or otherwise recall details from a previous conversation.

Ask you about yourself. He'll want to know more about you. If he doesn't do this, he may still be interested, but if he does, it's a good sign.

Talk about his possessions or achievements. Although this behavior can be amusing, it's a common way men try to impress women. Some men are obvious: one man I spoke to told me that the salary I make in a year was equivalent to just one of his bonuses (I was still a graduate student, and no, I did not go out with him!). Others are more subtle: another man casually mentioned right away that he was in a band, knowing that women like musicians.

Compliment you. This is always a good sign.

Seem nervous. Another very good sign. Look for fidgeting, stuttering, looking away when he talks to you, clearing his throat.

Indicate that he's single. He may mention his ex-girlfriend or that he lives alone. If you saw him with a woman, he'll be sure to state that she's a friend or family member.

Recognize you. If a man you talk to recognizes you from a class, restaurant, the gym, or pretty much anywhere, it's a good sign. It means he noticed you, and remembered you.

Ask you out. If a man seems interested but doesn't ask you out, he probably has a girlfriend. Or, he's shy and needs more encouragement.

Overall, reading body language and other signs of interest is an art that takes practice and experience. Don't get caught up in any specific sign that you see—it's more important to look for patterns of signs.

The ABCs of Initiating

Often, you'll instinctively feel when a man is interested in you, and once you know the signs, that instinct will improve. However, while men's interest is much clearer to women than women's interest is to men, there are no guarantees—sometimes you'll be wrong! It's all part of the learning experience. Either way, if you learn to read men, you'll increase your chances of connecting with men who interest you.

Know the Signs Cold

One of the first steps to initiating with a man is to learn and get a feel for signs a man is interested in you. As you learned, these signs show up in his body language, eye contact, and in how he talks to you. With experience, recognizing interest will become more instinctive. If you sense a man is checking you out, you can decide whether you're interested and go from there. If a guy is showing signs of interest, you have a very good chance of success with him if you do your part and initiate, using the strategies outlined here.

However, if you don't see signs of interest, or the signs are ambiguous, it doesn't necessarily mean you can't try to initiate with him. Sometimes a man's interest will be "jogged" when he finds out you're interested in him. Research has shown that we find people more attractive when we discover that they find us attractive. This is yet another reason why initiating is so powerful.

Laura worked with Jose at a restaurant. Laura was interested in Jose, but Jose was a quiet guy who kept to himself, and showed no signs of interest in her. Laura told a coworker that she found Jose attractive, and the coworker mentioned it to Jose. Jose then talked to Laura, and asked her out a week later. They're still together.

Send the Signal

To some extent, all women give off signs of interest to men without realizing it, but some women are subtler than others. Subtlety doesn't work with most men. If you want to get a guy's attention, send clear signals and give the green light that it's okay to approach you. This can be achieved by doing the following:

Look at men you find attractive. Let him see you look, even if briefly. If a man sees you looking, unless he's totally clueless, he will at least notice and possibly start showing signs of interest. But don't be too subtle—it may take looking at him three times to get him to do something. Don't stare, but make it clear you're checking him out.

Make eye contact. If you really want to get a man's attention, make eye contact with him. Unless you're bold, this won't be easy—eye contact is powerful stuff. If he immediately looks away and doesn't make any more eye contact, he isn't interested at that time. If he locks eyes with you, hold his eye contact for at least a couple of seconds. Then, a minute or two later, do it again. If he keeps looking, you may have a live one. Some men will nod or smile, and more outgoing men will say hello to you.

Smile. If eye contact gets a man's attention, a smile is often the green light he needs to talk to you. Smiling, even if not directly at him, shows that you're approachable and less likely to bite his head off or reject him.

Open up your body language. To make yourself seem approachable, keep a relaxed and pleasant look on your face. Don't cross your arms or legs. Orient your body toward the man you're interested in, and look at him. A smiling woman with open body language will get much more male attention than a serious woman with her arms crossed, looking at the floor.

Look accessible. The best way to look accessible is to be alone. This is *much* less intimidating for men. However, since you may not want to go to a bar or party by yourself, it's fine to be with one friend, preferably a woman. The worst thing is to be in a crowd of women. Guys are terrified of approaching a group of women, and only guys who are nuts (or drunk) will do it, usually with bad results. Also, position yourself for accessibility: at a bar, avoid corners or tables in the back. At a party, stay in the center of the room or near the food or drinks. At the gym, don't wear an iPod.

Okay, so now you know how to increase the chances of getting a man to approach you by initiating with body language. But what about unwanted attention? If you see a man checking you out and you're not interested in him, or you're just not in the mood to be bothered, do the opposite of everything above: avoid looking at him, and avoid all eye contact. Don't smile, and look a little annoyed. If possible, close off your body language by turning away from him or crossing your arms. Again, he won't think, "Oh, she isn't making eye contact, she must not be interested." He will just instinctively know to stay away.

Give Him an "In"

Many times, a guy will notice you and want to talk to you, but he struggles with what to say. Guys don't want to feel foolish, look like they're trying too hard, or resort to dumb pickup lines. So give him an "in," an excuse to make conversation.

Wear a T-shirt or hat with a message. Men read T-shirts and hats and will often comment on them. Voilà—instant conversation. You can wear your favorite sports team, college, the state you grew up in, or anything funny. I cannot tell you how many times men have commented on my T-shirts.

Laugh. Laughter can be even more powerful than smiling to encourage conversation with a man. For example, if you read something funny in the paper when you're in line for coffee, a man will want to know what's so funny. He'll feel okay asking because laughing people are happy, and more approachable.

Read an interesting or controversial book. If you're in a bookstore, coffee shop, or airport, men will notice what you're reading. If it's controversial, or a best-seller, it will inspire conversation more easily. Chick lit probably won't help you much.

Wear interesting clothing. Men notice interesting clothing and accessories more than you'd think. An unusual pair of boots, color of nail polish, or piece of jewelry might get his attention. Sometimes they're into the clothes, but usually it's just an excuse to talk to you.

Join clubs. Athletic groups (running clubs, cycling clubs, coed softball teams) have a built-in theme and will facilitate conversation easily. Men will feel more comfortable talking to you because you have something in common. Same with social events with a theme, such as Super

Bowl parties and birthday parties—he can ask you if you're a Broncos fan or how you know the birthday girl.

In my experience, you never know what men will comment on or notice. Even if it results in no dates, at least you'll enjoy an interesting conversation and get good practice conversing with a variety of men.

Chat It Up

Sometimes eye contact, smiling, and other tactics will get a guy's attention, but won't be enough to get him to actually talk to you. Here's a list of reasons he may need more encouragement:

He's been wrong in the past. Many men have experienced a woman giving off signs, just to find out she's not interested, just wants to be friends, or has a boyfriend. They get cautious and wait for more obvious signs before taking a risk.

He's shy. While most guys fear approaching women, some men are shy and not accustomed to starting conversations with strangers. These men need a bigger boost than other men. Often, you'll find that these men are nice guys who fear coming on too strong to women.

He's younger than you. As discussed in Mistake #6, younger men are much less likely to hit on older women, so initiating with conversation will help.

Difficult environment. Men are less likely to talk to you in places where socializing isn't typical or expected, such as the gym, the grocery store, or the bank. Contrary to popular myths about gyms being "meat markets," most men know to leave women alone there. Men don't want to be rejected or given the cold shoulder, especially in front of other men.

You're hot. Many guys are very intimidated by beautiful women and assume they already have a guy, can get a better guy than him, or are tired of being hit on. If you're tired of the guys who hit on you for your looks, think about talking to cute men who aren't as bold.

You're reserved. Reserved people are typically more introverted and have closed body language, which makes them appear less approachable. If people have told you that you look reserved or unapproachable, the burden is on you to initiate. Outgoing women have an easier time getting dates.

Overall, men may need more than nonverbal signals, particularly in certain situations. Breaking the sound barrier will establish your approachability, and his interest, once and for all. So how do you initiate conversation? Here are several ways:

Say hi. A simple hello will often break the ice. If he's someone you see regularly, a "How are you?" or "How's it going?" is a way to greet him without feeling like you're hitting on him. If he's interested in talking, he'll find something to talk about.

Ask for help. Ask a guy for the time, for directions, or for help with something that's quick. If you're at the gym, ask how to use a machine or for help with heavy weights. Men truly enjoy helping women, and if he likes you, he'll keep talking to you.

Compliment him. Men are used to giving compliments, but rarely receive them. I once complimented a guy on his shirt at a crowded party—we ended up talking the rest of the night. Because men aren't used to compliments, they may look away or otherwise not acknowledge the compliment. Don't be discouraged—as long as they're still talking to you, they're probably beaming on the inside.

Tell him you recognize him. If you're at a party and recognize a guy from your gym or coffee shop, say hi and tell him you know him from somewhere. The familiarity increases the chances that he will be polite and open to chatting.

Introduce yourself. This is a good way to initiate in situations where people are expected to exchange names, like social clubs, the workplace, or friends' parties. If you're new to an organization, introduce yourself to men and say you're new. If you've been a member of your ski club for years and a new man joins, say hello and introduce yourself to him.

The good thing about all of these suggestions is that they can be done in a friendly way that isn't forward, aggressive, or sexual. Even if he isn't interested, most men will be glad for some female attention, or at least for a friendly person during their long day.

Of course, initiating conversation with men isn't that difficult if you aren't that interested. If you are interested, it can be extremely intimidating, so much so that you may avoid talking to them altogether! If you've ever felt this way, that should give you an idea of what men have to face. Here are a few pointers to deal with this obstacle:

Practice. Practice initiating conversation with strangers who don't make you nervous, such as women and children. Move on to older men, teenage boys, and men who don't interest you, then to men who do interest you. It will get easier with time.

Don't hesitate. When you see an opening for conversation, take it. The longer you wait, the more likely you'll over-think it and become nervous. If you like the guy's leather jacket, just say so.

Keep it short. If you keep the comment quick, you'll feel less nervous. He'll also feel more comfortable, knowing you aren't some weird girl who will talk his ear off. You can say, "Cool shirt," smile, and go back to picking out vegetables or ordering your coffee. He may take up the reins and continue the conversation, either then or next time he sees you.

Act blasé. Try to start a conversation as if it's no big deal, like something you do every day. If you do this enough times, it won't be a big deal. Of course, if he shows signs of interest, you can always step it up a notch.

Overall, if you talk to him and he doesn't seem that interested, at least you've done the toughest thing: broken the ice. If you see him again, it will be that much easier for him to talk to you. By that time, he may be more interested or more ready to talk. If he does seem interested, there's a good chance he'll ask you out or get your number. If he doesn't ask for it, you're faced with a decision: move on, or initiate at the next level by making a move.

Make a Move

If you have good initial contact with a guy and sense he's interested, but he doesn't take the next step by getting your info, you can give him your number or suggest getting together sometime. Some women will say you should never give out a number or suggest getting together; but your instincts and intuition are better instruments than a set of rigid rules. Do what feels right to you. If you try and nothing comes of it, you can move on to someone else. Over time, you will get better at knowing when to make a move, and when to let him do the asking. If he fails to close the deal, he either has a girlfriend, is unsure of himself, or isn't sure he's interested yet. If you meet him in a setting where you will have future contact with him, you have the luxury of waiting to see if he'll make a move later.

So what if you're dating online? Then, making a move is simple. Instead of waiting for men to e-mail you, many of whom won't be your type, just pick some men who you find attractive and interesting, and e-mail them. Greet them by their name or handle, mention something you found interesting in their profile, and say "let me know if you're interested." One woman I know uses this method exclusively. She's gotten about a 70 percent response rate, and gets to date the men who interest her.

A Few Words of Warning

There's a difference between initiating and pursuing. Women initiate, and men pursue. Initiating is starting things, giving men the green light to proceed. Once you've initiated in the ways I talk about above, he'll take it from there or he won't. If he doesn't, your work is done—move on to someone else. For example, if you make eye contact with a man a few times and he doesn't respond much or show signs of interest, stop looking his way. If you talk to a man and he doesn't seem interested in talking, politely excuse yourself and don't approach him again. If he does seem interested and you give him your number, but he doesn't call, write him off.

Never pursue a man. All you need to do is clearly show him your interest, and he'll pursue you. If he doesn't, he isn't interested, and if he isn't interested, you're wasting your time if you do any more than that. And remember: a man has no control over his interest level, so try not to take it personally.

Another thing to keep in mind is that initiating is not sexual. Initiating is as simple as making contact with a man and showing him you're receptive to his attention. In fact, many of these techniques can work well in nondating social situations, where you want to meet new people. You aren't coming on to men and so most won't "get the wrong idea."

One more warning: As I've said, eye contact and other nonverbal signs of interest are not always conscious. When a guy signals interest, it doesn't necessarily mean he's available. Unfortunately, sometimes partnered or married men will send signals. These men may be looking to cheat, or may be just looking around with no intention of acting on their feelings. Often, these men won't go further than eye contact.

> Grace frequented the same coffee house for years, and recognized a lot of the regular customers. A cute guy often checked her out and made strong eye contact with her, but never talked to her. She decided to initiate conversation with him one day. After that, he would go out of his way to come talk to her, and seemed very interested. After several conversations, he mentioned his wife. Grace was surprised that he was married, but she said nothing and stopped paying attention to him.

If you don't know him, it's even more important to be cautious. While some partnered men looking to cheat will actively pursue women, most send out signals and wait for women to come to them. Partnered men who stare at, make eye contact with, or flirt with other women are treading into dangerous waters. This is not the same as briefly looking at other women, which is pretty much harmless if done discreetly and without signs of interest. If you initiate with a man who's giving you signs and he turns out to be married, walk away.

The Final Word

Despite how important it is for you to initiate, most women resist doing so or feel intimidated by the task. Women tend to have specific fears about making contact with men. Here are some of these fears, followed by why there is no need to let that fear stop you.

Fear: If I initiate with a man, he'll think I'm aggressive or desperate.

Reality: Pursuing or coming on to him sexually is aggressive. Initiating is only indicating approachability or potential interest, and shows confidence, not desperation. He'll feel flattered, if not relieved.

Fear: If I initiate with a man, I won't know if he's truly interested.

Reality: The signs of interest (listed earlier in this section) are the same whether you initiate or he does. Once you smile at or talk to a man, that will give him the opportunity to show his interest if he hasn't already.

Fear: If I ask a man out, he'll think I'm chasing him.

Reality: While calling a man or asking him out is a gutsier form of initiating, it isn't chasing if you only do it one time. And most men don't mind being asked out.

Fear: I don't want to feel obligated to go out with men I initiate with.

Reality: Initiating is only making contact and creating an opportunity. Neither of you has to take the opportunity. Sometimes it's fun to just talk. In fact, you'll find that the just-chat scenario will happen often.

Fear: If I initiate with a man, what happens if he has a girlfriend or doesn't show interest in me?

Reality: You're only making contact with him. If he's unavailable or uninterested, you'll still feel good for having tried, and you've opened up the possibility for the future in case his relationship doesn't work out or he becomes interested in you. Also, many men, particularly shy or reserved men, won't show interest right away.

Fear: I'm afraid if I initiate with a man, he'll reject me or blow me off.

Reality: If you follow the advice in this section, that will rarely happen. Even if he's not interested, he'll probably be polite, even flattered by your interest. If he's rude or blows you off, always remember that his behavior is about him, not you. And, if you feel this fear, you now understand the fear single men deal with every day.

As you can see, fear is the main reason women don't initiate. Because making contact with men can be scary, it's often easier to pass the buck and expect men to do all the work. Remember the woman I mentioned at the beginning of this section, who e-mailed me and said my Gym Cutie had no balls? Somehow it was okay for me to be a coward, but not him! You can live in fear if you choose, but you'll miss a lot of good opportunities with men. Wouldn't you prefer to do that small thing and have some say in who you date? That's the way nature intended it.

Overall, initiating things with men is a powerful way to make your dating life more fun and successful. You call the shots, pick the men you want, and greatly increase the chances of dating men you want to date instead of waiting for them to come to you. Yes, initiating does involve risk—but you will find that succeeding in any area of life requires you to take risks. Go ahead and initiate; you'll be glad you did.

Mistake #8

You Ignore the Red Flags

> "Too many people ignore the yellow alerts because paying attention to them would require them to do something that is uncomfortable."

> JACK CANFIELD, *THE SUCCESS PRINCIPLES*

One of the most annoying aspects of dating is that people like to show their best selves up front, and you don't always know what you're getting into until it's too late. You know what I'm talking about—the guy who's sweet and totally cool at first, making you all fluttery for him, and once you start to care for him, he turns into a total ass. Wouldn't it be nice to be able to spot guys like that right away? Well, you can—maybe not every time, but much more often than you think.

The thing is, for every problem you've had with a guy you've dated, there was almost always some sign at the beginning that he was NOT the right guy. These early signs are known as red flags. Some say that you can learn all you need to know about a man in three dates. Sometimes you can find out even sooner. If you want a good guy, a keeper, don't invest time and energy into men who aren't likely to give you what you need. The trick is to learn to recognize the early signs that a guy is a poor investment, and move on to someone better.

In this section, you'll learn the Top 10 red flags to look for when you meet a new guy, and how to detect them. Although there are many types of men to avoid, this section focuses on the most common red flags women miss early on. Most of these red flags can be spotted within the first three dates, if not sooner.

Red Flag #1:
He's Not Interested Enough

This is the first red flag because it's one of the most common and it creates a lot of confusion among women. Fortunately, a few guidelines make this red flag relatively easy to spot.

Why would a woman bother with a guy who isn't showing interest in her? Lots of reasons. For one, some women are inexperienced. With time, detecting interest (and lack of it) becomes much easier. Two, it's a lot easier to see a lack of interest when it isn't happening to you! And finally, the biggest reason women don't always see this red flag is because some men send mixed messages, showing both signs of interest and disinterest at the same time. First, let's go over the basic signs that he's not interested.

He Doesn't Call

Asking for your number and then not calling is probably one of the most baffling things men do. Men typically call under two conditions: he's interested in you, and he believes you're interested in him. Condition #1 is most important, but never dismiss the importance of Condition #2. Men have many reasons for not following through with a phone call, but these reasons tend to fall into three categories:

Game playing. These men want the challenge of getting your number or want to prove to their friends (and themselves) that they have game. They're typically young and immature. Game players are common in bars and clubs, and they aren't serious about dating.

Not enough interest. These men feel interest initially, but after considering things, change their minds. It takes time for two people to develop interest and to feel comfortable calling. Certain circumstances don't allow for that time. This is why a phone number given out at a bar or grocery store (i.e., places where you don't have much time to get acquainted) won't always result in a call. He's more likely to call if you met at work, school, or through friends—settings where you have time to get comfortable around each other and make sure the interest is there. It's also possible he didn't call because he met someone else.

Doubts about your interest. Some men assume you're interested if you give your number, but many won't call unless they know you want them to. Guys, like everyone, are more interested in someone who is interested in them. Remember: for every guy who's gathered a number and not called, there's a woman who's given out her number, screened the call, and not called back.

He Doesn't Follow Up

If a guy doesn't call you within three days after a date, he's not interested at that time. Think about it: If you like someone and have a great time with them, you aren't going to just forget about them—you're going to follow up in order to book the next date, before they lose interest or find someone else. He should also make clear plans to see you again. An interested man will ask you out at the end of a date, or call you within a couple of days and ask you. Finally, he isn't interested if he cancels a date without rescheduling, no matter what the reason.

Don't waste time with men who aren't showing signs of interest. If you're interested in a guy and see any of the above signs—and you will if you're dating—the best plan is to forget about him and move on. Don't make excuses for him (e.g., he's busy or under a lot of stress). The man you're looking for will overlook these issues and make an effort.

The above signs are clear indicators that a guy isn't interested. But what about situations that aren't so clear? You know, the situations where a guy shows enough interest to make you hold out hope, but not enough for you to feel sure? Consider these scenarios:

- Melinda met Rory at a coffee house. Melinda picked up strong signs of interest from Rory, but told Rory she was extremely busy studying for the Bar exam. They exchanged numbers, and Rory said they should meet up when she finishes her exam. Melinda decided that Rory wouldn't remember to call in a month, so she called him. They had a great conversation, but she did not hear from Rory after that.
- Caroline and Jay met at a mutual friend's party. They talked much of the evening. Jay contacted Caroline via e-mail and suggested meeting for a movie. They enjoyed themselves, and talked until late. After that night, Jay didn't call Caroline for two weeks, but then asked her out again.
- Maria met Joey at a neighborhood bar. After four months of dating, they see each other once a week. When Christmas came around, Joey went to visit his family, and he and Maria did not exchange gifts.

Each of these scenarios shows signs of interest and dis-interest. However, each scenario has enough information for each woman to know how to proceed despite the guys' mixed signals. Here are some examples of mixed signals, and how to handle them:

He calls, but not often. Calling is a sign of interest, but calling infrequently isn't. Just when you've given up on a guy, he calls. If he isn't calling you on a regular basis, move on.

He says he'll call and then doesn't. Lack of follow-through is a sign of weak interest, not to mention a sign of flaki-ness. This is true even if he eventually calls.

He e-mails or text messages. E-mail is fine initially, but once you've gone out, e-mails and texts should be *additional* ways to stay in touch, not the primary ways.

Your dates are infrequent. While it's good to take things slowly at the start, they should pick up pace after a while if you're interested in each other. After several dates, a guy who takes you out once a week or less isn't showing enough interest. It doesn't matter if he's consumed with work or other obligations.

He's still seeing other women. Regardless of how inter-ested he seems, once you've gone out several times, he isn't overly interested if he's still seeing other women.

Your relationship is mostly sexual. You may see a man on a regular basis and he may call you, but if you spend most of your time together having sex rather than going out and getting to know each other, sex is probably his main interest. If this is all you want, enjoy. But if he isn't trying to get more than sex from you, then he isn't interested beyond sex.

He puts his friends first. A man should spend plenty of time with his friends, even if he has a girlfriend. However, a man who wants to be with his friends more than you isn't that interested. The same is true if he doesn't introduce you to his friends.

So, after reading this section, how should the women in each of these scenarios handle her situation?

Rory showed interest by exchanging numbers with Melinda and talking to her when she called, but didn't pick up the ball and call or ask her out once Melinda made her interest known. Rory isn't interested enough and Melinda should move on.

Jay showed interest by asking Caroline out again, but he waited way too long to call. He may not be that interested, or is seeing other women. Caroline could see Jay again if she feels comfortable. But if he doesn't pick up the pace after the second date, Caroline should move on.

Joey sees Maria once a week and they've dated for four months, but their relationship hasn't picked up speed and he didn't give Maria a Christmas gift. Joey is not serious about Maria. If she wants more, she needs to move on.

Overall, don't bother with men who don't show genuine interest. If, however, you don't mind a more casual arrangement where you see other people or don't talk that often, enjoy yourself. Dating is about finding what you want, whatever it may be. But if you want something more and find yourself in a mixed-signals situation, walk away and hold out for something better. Too many women don't recognize this red flag and waste their time.

Finally, beware of a guy who, once you walk away from the situation, suddenly seems interested. I've seen men try to convince a woman that they care after not calling her. I've seen men pay no attention to a woman and then get jealous if she dates another guy. These men are usually jerks who want you to put up with their crap. Ultimately, you choose whether or not to give him one more chance and see if he resumes his old ways.

So why do men bother with women if they don't have serious intentions? Because they get something out of having you around, and assume you're cool with the arrangement because you agree to it. As they say, it takes two to tango.

The take-home message here is to not waste your time with guys who aren't interested at the same level you are. Instead, focus on genuinely interested men. So what does a genuinely interested man look like?

He calls you. If a man is interested in you, he will call, and call often. This is one of the most telling signs of interest in a man. If you give him your number, he calls you. If he takes you out, he calls you within a couple of days. After you've gone out a few times, he calls you regularly. Some say that if a man calls you every day, he's in love; in my experience, this is true.

He wants to see you. An interested man will want to see you. He will take you out and then book the next date with you, or he will call soon after your date to make more plans with you. He will make time in his schedule for you, and he will often choose to be with you over being with his friends.

He isn't interested in seeing other women. Once he's gotten to know you, a truly interested man will not want to see other women.

He includes you. When a man likes you, he will introduce you to his friends and his family. He will include you in activities that involve them. Often, they will indicate that he's told them about you; for example, they will say, "It's nice to finally meet you."

If you're interested in a guy you've been dating, look for these signs. Know them, expect them, and don't settle for less. Not only will you enjoy dating more, but you'll be investing your time and energy into men who have real potential.

One note of caution: as you learned in Mistake #3, a guy's lack of interest, no matter how disappointing, is due to factors that he (and you) have no control over. Maybe the two C's weren't there, or the timing was off. Once you see the signs, your first reaction should be, "This isn't working for me," rather than, "There's something wrong with me." Ultimately, a guy is either right for you or he isn't.

Red Flag #2:
Weak Chemistry

In Mistake #2, you learned about chemistry and its role in creating interest and attraction. Sometimes you'll meet a man who has the qualities you're looking for, who you may really like, but you just don't "feel it" with him. Here are some signs that the chemistry isn't there:

- You like him but don't feel tingly or nervous around him
- You don't worry about looking your best around him
- You don't look forward to having sex with him, or have a hard time imagining sex with him
- You don't look forward to talking to him or going out with him
- You're still actively checking out other guys
- You find yourself feeling annoyed with him
- If he's a great guy, you have to keep talking yourself into him

Feelings of strong chemistry with a guy can happen right away or they can take some time to develop. However, you need to feel some chemistry within the first couple of dates with a guy. Otherwise, your interest level won't be high enough. And if you keep dating, your relationship will lack passion and it will be like dating a good friend. Chemistry alone won't sustain a relationship, but it's a necessary component for a successful one. While it's a good idea to give a quality guy a chance, don't waste your time with a man you don't feel good chemistry with.

Red Flag #3: Low Compatibility

You've also learned about the importance of compatibility and its role in your attraction to a guy. Compatibility is when a guy has the qualities you're looking for. Compatibility doesn't hit you in the obvious way that chemistry does, but it's just as important. A relationship with good chemistry but low compatibility will crash and burn. While truly good compatibility is difficult to see when you first start dating someone, certain types of incompatibility are easy to see up front. Here are some things to consider when you meet a guy:

Lifestyle, interests, and hobbies. Look for things like smoking, drinking, eating, and exercise habits—are they what you're looking for? How does he spend his spare time? If he travels, where does he go? Is he more of a sports nut or a refined artsy type? Is he career-oriented or is his job just a means to enjoy his hobbies? If you love to party and go out on the town, you may want to avoid men who prefer to stay home and read. If you're outdoorsy, you want him to be too. If you enjoy cultural activities like theater and art, hopefully he does too. You don't have to be the same, but avoid guys who differ too much from you in this area.

Values. When you peruse a guy's online profile or chat with him on a date, the things he mentions often indicate the things that matter most to him. Does he talk about family? His passion for rock climbing? His involvement with church? His career? You want a guy with similar values to yours.

His personality. Everyone is different, and everyone clicks with a different type of personality. Consider things like whether he's serious or silly, outgoing or shy, a leader or more laid back, and so on. You want a guy whose personality you click with, not clash with.

Whether he has kids. Some women prefer to date men who have no kids, whereas others don't mind either way. Some prefer men with kids, particularly if they have kids themselves. A single parent can understand the challenges another single parent faces.

Whether either of you wants kids. You can't really ask this question right away, but often it will come up. If you're dating online, pay close attention to this criterion. Don't date anyone who doesn't want what you want on this crucial item.

The type of relationship he wants. People date for different reasons—some want only sex, some want a casual relationship, others want marriage. Incompatibility in this area is very common, yet many overlook it when they date. Often, guys will drop hints about this when you first meet them, so pay close attention. Don't date a guy who doesn't want what you do and hope he'll change his mind.

It's important to know what you must have in a man and what you're more flexible on—see Mistake #4 on this topic. No matter how cute he is or how good the chemistry is, don't compromise on compatibility. He may be a good guy, but not the guy for you.

Red Flag #4:
He's Only Looking for Sex

As mentioned earlier, people date for different reasons, and it's crucial that you date someone who wants the same type of relationship you want. You can usually tell pretty quickly when a man is primarily interested in sex.

There's nothing wrong with only wanting sex. The problem arises when a guy only wants sex and you believe he wants more. Most men aren't up front about only wanting sex, so you have to read between the lines. Here are a few signs that he only wants sex:

He makes sexual remarks. All guys are interested in sex. But a guy who's interested in more than sex won't bring up sexual topics or make sexual innuendos too soon because he knows he'll risk offending you or turning you off. He knows to avoid that topic until it's appropriate. So avoid men who talk about sex right away. If you bring up sex, however, he may feel he has the green light to talk about it or even to make moves on you!

He makes moves on you right away. Men who do anything more than try to kiss you on a first date are looking primarily for sex. Again, men may want more, but they won't usually try for more if they are interested in getting to know you.

He wants to go to his, or your, place right away. It's pretty difficult to have sex in restaurants, coffee shops, bars, or other places where dates happen. If you just met him and he wants to go to your place or his, he wants sex. Avoid each other's homes until you know he wants more than sex.

He pressures you. Never trust a man who pressures you for sex. A good guy will respect your boundaries and back off if you say no.

You don't hear from him. If a guy wants to have sex and then you don't hear from him, he was only interested in sex, regardless of whether you said yes or no to his request. A man who's interested in getting to know you would never lose interest because you said no to sex.

He booty-calls you. When a man calls late and wants to come over, it isn't a date or a sign of interest, it's a call for sex. A guy who wants more will take you out.

You meet him at a bar. It's possible to meet a good guy at a bar and we all know happy couples who've met at bars. But many people, especially men, associate bars with drinking and hooking up. Many people go to bars for that purpose, as many bartenders will tell you. If you meet an interesting guy in a bar, make sure he's a gentleman that night and beyond.

If a man is attracted to you, he will want to have sex with you, period. However, if he's interested in more than sex, he'll wait and spend time getting to know you. Men who only want sex are impatient, and will disappear if they don't get what they want.

Red Flag #5:
He's Not Ready for a Relationship

If you're looking for a serious relationship, and certainly if you're interested in getting married, you'll want to avoid men who aren't where you are. Look for these signs:

He's young. While many men in the eighteen to twenty-four age bracket are capable of relationships, men this age are the least likely to want to get serious, and the most likely to cheat or do other dog-like things. In terms of marriage, the average man in the United States doesn't marry until he's twenty-seven. Educated men marry later. Men have told me that, in their twenties, they dated women they could have married but didn't because they weren't ready yet.

He needs to find himself. Men who don't know what they want out of life, don't seem to have goals or direction, or aren't happy with their lives, aren't ready for the real thing. They make poor partners because they aren't happy with themselves.

He's on the rebound. Watch out for a guy who just got out of a relationship or marriage. He'll pursue you like crazy and swear he's ready for a relationship, and then complain about his ex all the time or pull a bait-and-switch, where he comes on strong and then pushes you away. Wait until he's been on his own for a while.

He has a history of short relationships. If a guy has no long, serious relationships under his belt, there's usually a reason. The older he gets, the truer this is.

He says negative things about relationships or marriage. Men who say they aren't ready for marriage, or that they "might want it someday," aren't great investments if you want marriage. Ditto for men who say marriage is overrated, or who complain that their ex-girlfriends pressured them to get married. Some will be direct, others indirect, but when a man is negative on marriage, take him seriously.

Overall, avoid investing in men who are unlikely to give you the relationship you want, no matter what their age or status.

Red Flag #6:
He's a Jerk

Have you ever met a cool guy you really liked, just to have him turn into a total jerk once you got to know him better? Not a fun experience. A jerk can put on a good face for a while. But if you look closely, there are usually signs he's a jerk before he shows his bad side, and you can often see them more quickly than you'd think. Here are some signs that a guy is a jerk:

He's negative. We all make negative comments about others from time to time. But it's something we do around friends or people we trust. If a guy says negative things right away or on the first few dates, it's a bad sign. I briefly dated a guy who told me how lazy his employees were and how back-stabbing his boss was—on our second date. Sure enough, after a couple more dates, he turned out to be a jerk. Also, watch out for men who badmouth their exes. No matter how nuts she is, how he talks about her is a preview of how he'll treat you. A guy can dislike his ex and disapprove of her behavior without disparaging her.

He doesn't respect your time. A quality man respects others' time. He shows up on time and follows through on phone calls and dates. If he can't make it, he lets you know. Check out this example: Lilly met John online and he asked her out for dinner. Since they were both leaving town for the weekend, they scheduled their date for the following Tuesday and agreed that they'd decide on a place later. Lilly got back into town, but Tuesday evening rolled around and she had not heard from John. Lilly e-mailed John, wondering if something had happened.

John replied Wednesday and apologized; he said that something else had come up, and to him, their date was not confirmed.

Anytime you agree on a day to do something with a man, it's a date, whether the details are ironed out or not. If John had simply e-mailed Lilly and said he couldn't make it, he would've been a disinterested man rather than a jerk. Don't bother with men who don't follow through with phone calls or dates. A lack of follow-through is disrespectful and a sign of immaturity and poor manners.

He's rude to others. You know the old adage: the way a man treats other people is the way he'll treat you down the road. Pay particular attention to how he treats service people, including waitresses and store clerks.

He's rude to you. If a guy is rude to you when you meet him or go out with him, don't walk, RUN away. This is a sign of extreme insecurity and only a taste of what's to come. Obviously, criticism or angry behavior is unacceptable. But beware of more subtle rudeness, such as making jokes about your behavior or appearance. If you're unsure if a man's humor is rude, trust your instincts. Did you laugh, or feel offended, hurt, or confused? Humor is a common tool that insecure men use to feel more powerful.

He isn't a gentleman. Chivalry and good manners aren't as common as they used to be. A lack of chivalry doesn't necessarily mean a guy is a jerk. Some men, especially young men, just don't know better. However, bad manners or an unwillingness to be a gentleman when you ask him nicely is a bad sign. A guy should pick you up on the first few dates. He should open the door for you. He should walk you to your car or your door to make sure you get home safely. If you go to his home, he should try to make you feel comfortable. If you run into his friends, he should introduce you. Gentlemanly behavior is not about treating women like they're helpless; it's a way that a man shows he's generous and thinks of others besides himself.

Dating is a time when people are supposed to be on their best behavior—if a guy's already doing the above behaviors, you don't even want to know what things will be like down the road. Some experts say to give a guy three strikes—if he screws up three times, he's out. I disagree. In my experience, a guy who shows jerky behavior never turns out to be a good guy if you get to know him better. So jerks only get one strike. Ditch him and move on to a better man.

Deception

Another type of jerky behavior worth mentioning is deception. Deception involves either lying or neglecting to reveal the truth at a time when it would be appropriate to reveal it. Here are two examples where men showed deceptive behavior:

Tina met Jeff on an online dating site. In his profile, Jeff stated that he was divorced. They decided to meet for dinner. They hit it off, and Jeff asked Tina to go out again. On their second date, Jeff revealed that he was not divorced yet, but still in the process of getting divorced.

Corinne met Joshua at a professional conference. They talked and found they had some things in common. However, they lived in different states. Joshua liked Corinne and e-mailed her after they went their separate ways. He flirted with her over e-mail, and suggested she attend an upcoming conference with him so he could take her out. Corinne Googled Joshua and found out that he was married with kids.

Both Jeff and Joshua were intentionally deceptive. Despite the fact that "separated" is an option on his online profile, Jeff lied by selecting "divorced" because he knew fewer women would want to date a separated man. There's a good reason for this—as I discuss in *Dating the Divorced Man*, separated men are a risky bunch.

Joshua was also deceptive: he deliberately neglected to mention his family during their conversations because he knew Corinne probably would have blown him off if she'd known he was married.

Unfortunately, deception is common in men. Some men deceive because they believe it's the only way to get what they want, and because they care more about getting what they want than they do about other people. This type of guy will hide the truth in the desperate hope that a woman will fall for him or sleep with him before she finds out the real story. Social scientists call this the Foot-in-the-Door Phenomenon: if a man can get a woman to go out with him by hiding the truth, he gets his "foot in the door," and if she likes him she is more likely to agree to keep seeing him after the truth comes out. The problem is, deception is manipulative and shows a lack of integrity.

Online dating is also a hotbed of deception. Some men exaggerate their height or income, or display a photo representing a younger or thinner version of themselves. These men don't feel they're good enough as they are. While this type of deception is irritating, it's much less destructive than the above examples; plus, you'll find out the truth on your first meeting, and you can decide then how to handle it.

How truthful should a man be? The more the truth would influence a woman's desire to date him, the sooner he should be honest. For example, married and partnered men should be honest about that right away. Men still going through a divorce should admit that within the first couple of dates, and should be honest in their profiles if dating online.

In my research, and my personal experience, deceptive men rarely turn out to be worthwhile guys.

Red Flag #7: He's Unavailable

If you're interested in meeting a great guy, he needs to be available. An available guy is not only single (that means no wife or girlfriend!), but also accessible to you. Here are signs that he isn't available, at least at that time:

He works all the time. Relationships require that you spend time together. You can't have a real relationship with a guy who works day and night.

He's seeing other people. You can date a guy who's seeing other women, but you can't have a relationship with him. He's unavailable.

He lives far away. Long Distance Relationships (LDRs) can work, but only if you talk to and see each other on a regular basis. If you're going to get serious, you'll eventually need to live in the same city.

He just split up with someone. This one's a hard one because he's technically available. But if he just broke up, he's going to be in pain and on the rebound. Rebounding men are often needy and selfish. Just give this one some time.

He's getting divorced but still living in the same house as his wife. Any guy sharing a home with an ex isn't available, even if he's sleeping in the basement. If he were ready to date, he'd move out and start his own life.

Red Flag #8:
He's Emotionally Unavailable

Unlike the unavailable man, an emotionally unavailable man is technically available, but he keeps an emotional blockade up, never letting you in and never allowing the closeness that has to occur for a relationship to be happy and fulfilling. This guy keeps you at arm's length. Be warned that this is the toughest red flag to pick up on up front; it may take several dates to see it, and will often take longer than that. And even when you do get the full brunt of it, you may not recognize it right away. But the sooner you do, the better, because an emotionally unavailable man will drive you crazy. Here are the signs that he may fall into this category:

He's always busy with work. An emotionally unavailable man will use work as an excuse for keeping you at arm's length. These men are always too "busy" or "exhausted" to give you much of themselves. A man who's emotionally available and interested in you will make time for you and be able to connect with you emotionally.

He lives far away. Geographical distance doesn't necessarily mean emotional distance. However, emotionally unavailable men often seek out LDRs because the geographical distance gives them the emotional distance they need. Be careful of a guy who lives far away and watch for other signs of emotional unavailability.

He calls infrequently. An emotionally available guy will call regularly, and you'll rarely wonder why he hasn't called. The emotionally unavailable guy will always keep you wondering, and he'll call too little or too late, after you're already annoyed.

He's hard to reach. When you call him or need him, he doesn't answer, takes too long to return your call, or doesn't come through for you.

He does the push-pull. An emotionally unavailable man will push you away or seem distant when you're available to him; but when you give up and distance yourself, he'll miraculously become caring and affectionate. This type of hot-cold behavior is a very bad sign.

He's "working through issues." If a guy uses his issues with his job, his life, his ex, etc., as an excuse for not being ready for a relationship or not being able to connect with you, he's emotionally unavailable. Issues are part of life and most guys just deal with them.

You feel uncomfortable. This is the most telltale sign. Things won't feel "right" when you date an emotionally unavailable man. You won't feel comfortable or secure. You'll think it's you, that you're needy. But if he's emotionally unavailable, your feelings are natural. You may not recognize your discomfort, so if you've dated a guy who didn't hold back emotionally, try to remember how it felt. Use that as a basis of comparison.

He says you have the problem. If you confront him about his emotional unavailability, it's likely that this man will tell you you're asking too much, are needy and insecure, and that you have the problem. He's right, you do have a problem: you want more than he's giving you. So go find it with someone else.

Nine times out of ten, you'll have to dump the emotionally unavailable man because he won't end things. He's comfortable with a limited relationship as long as you'll accept it. But an emotionally unavailable man can't make any woman happy.

Red Flag #9: He's Got Problems

Entire books have been written on Problem Guys. Here, I'll list some common signs to look for when you meet a guy. Fortunately, you can see these signs pretty quickly if you pay close attention.

Substance abusers. If he drinks more than two drinks on a date or talks a lot about drinking, he's probably got an alcohol problem. If he mentions that he smokes pot now and again, he probably smokes it regularly. Substance abusers have big problems, so avoid them.

Moody guys. If he shows any sign of moody, negative, or angry behavior when you date him, look out. Those are strong signs of problems that will get much worse.

Loners. Watch out for a guy who has no friends or isn't very social. Usually, there's a reason.

Poor-me guys. If he complains about his problems or goes on about how unfair life is, it's a sign that he's a victim. Everybody has problems or hard times, but healthy men do something about them.

Unemployment. While anyone can lose their job or get laid off, lack of employment can be a sign of serious problems. Make sure he's actively looking for a job and is responsible in other areas of his life.

Red Flag #10: You Have Bad Vibes

Sometimes, you meet a guy and for one reason or another, it just doesn't feel right. Maybe he shows one of the other red flags, but maybe not. Maybe he makes you feel bad, sad, or icky within the first few dates. Maybe you don't trust him or have a funny feeling about him. Whatever it is, you may not know the reason but you should listen to your feelings. Chances are, it's a red flag of some sort.

If something doesn't feel right when you date, you can analyze it six ways to Sunday, but ultimately you just have to ask yourself, "Does this feel good to me? Is this what I want?" Usually, if you have to ask yourself if it feels right, it probably doesn't. Especially if you have to ask these questions more than once. You'll learn more about trusting your instincts in Mistake #10.

Investing in the wrong men not only results in pain and disappointment, but it also wastes your precious time and prevents you from finding Mr. Right. When it comes to dating, a huge source of power comes from your ability to choose. You don't have power over men or over how they behave, but you can always choose which men you talk to, which men you go out with, how involved you get, and whether to walk away if your needs aren't met. You don't necessarily have to dump a guy immediately because he shows a red flag, depending on what he does. But do take note of it, take your time, and pay close attention to see if it's a real problem or no big deal.

Mistake #9

You Plan Your Wedding after the First Date

> "A lady's imagination is very rapid; it jumps from admiration to love, from love to matrimony in a moment."
>
> JANE AUSTEN, FROM *PRIDE AND PREJUDICE*

Have you ever heard a woman say any of the following things? Just as importantly, have *you* ever said any of them?

- "I just met my future husband."
- "I knew he was The One the moment I saw him!"
- "I'm the girl for him; he just doesn't know it yet . . ."
- "I know we barely know each other, but it's meant to be."

What do all these comments have in common? They all come from women who've come down with a case of One-itis. Oneitis is a condition that has plagued every woman at one time or another: you become hung up on one guy, as if he's the only guy in the universe, before you know much (or anything) about him.

The term "Oneitis," literally "illness from one," actually comes from the male pickup artist community. Pickup artists attempt to master the art of meeting and seducing women. They're like players in training. But no matter how skilled they become, once in a while they'll become infatuated with one particular girl. She'll become his focus to the exclusion of other girls, and he'll start behaving in ways that go against his player rulebook. Pickup artists fear Oneitis because they know it will kill their game and that they'll wind up turning off the object of their Oneitis with their puppy-dog infatuation.

Okay, so maybe you think players are dopes, or worse. Maybe you think it wouldn't kill these guys to stop playing games and date one girl at a time. Fine. But when a pickup artist settles down with one woman, it's because he chooses to, not because he gets a case of Oneitis. If he gets Oneitis, he doesn't get the girl because he turns her off by coming on too strong. Not surprisingly, it works the same way for women.

A case of Oneitis, if left untreated, can scare men away. It can also lead to disappointment and get you involved with the wrong guys for the wrong reasons. And while pickup artists fear Oneitis, the truth is that women are more prone to it than men are. This section will show you what Oneitis is, how to prevent it, and how to treat it if you catch it.

What Causes Oneitis?

There's an old stereotype that women fantasize about romance while men fantasize about sex. In reality, men and women care about both things, and everyone is different in their romantic and sexual needs. However, this stereotype has some truth when we first meet someone we like. Generally speaking, when a guy meets a girl, he experiences feelings of physical or sexual attraction first, and then, if he likes her, develops emotional or romantic ones second. Women tend to develop romantic feelings first, then sexual ones, or develop both at the same time. There's nothing wrong with this tendency, but it can cause problems.

A woman will imagine herself married to or in a serious gig with a guy before she knows anything about him. She'll imagine their kids, their home, and their life together. She develops a nice romantic fantasy based on a few things she's learned about the guy—if he's a doctor, she imagines him saving lives and then coming home to their big house with the three-car garage, having dinner with her, and tucking in Timmy, Tommy, and Tina at bedtime. These elaborate fantasies can happen extremely quickly, after talking to a guy, or after one date with him. If they click, she may wonder if he's the man for her. Meanwhile, this guy hasn't even begun considering these things yet—he's probably wondering what she looks like naked!

Okay, before you start to feel like I'm picking on you, I will say that fantasizing, like the three-car-garage woman did, is very common and very normal. In fact, sometimes you have no control over these types of thoughts and fantasies! You're having lunch with some guy you barely know, it's going great, and next thing you know you're imagining yourself married and walking on the beach together! A new guy can make you feel giddy. That's not the problem.

The problem is that sometimes, women take these fantasies too literally. Some women believe that these feelings and fantasies mean that she's met Mr. Right. But what they really mean is that she's strongly attracted to him. He could be The One, but he may not be. While many great romances started out with a strong "feeling" about a guy right from the beginning, there are many other times when that strong feeling goes nowhere at all and he turns out to be a frog rather than a prince. You can't know for sure until you put the time in and get to know each other.

So that's part of what causes Oneitis: women's tendency to romanticize mixed with feelings of strong attraction. Another cause is that many women are ready for a relationship or for marriage, and so they try to rush through dating to get what they want. Put all these factors together, and voilà!—the affliction takes over like a bad cold. And Hollywood doesn't help either: movies are filled with "love at first sight" and "I just knew" stuff because it's romantic and entertaining. It sells. And why not? We all love romance.

In the real world, however, romance has to be mixed with caution and patience. Dating, with all its annoyances, is a necessary step to finding the right person, and it cannot be rushed. No matter how good your attitude is or how good your taste in men, if you get too loopy over a guy you hardly know and develop a case of Oneitis, your dating life will suffer.

So now you know what Oneitis is and what causes it. Next, you'll learn about the most common types of Oneitis —and how to avoid coming down with a case yourself.

He's-The-One Syndrome (HTOS)

A woman suffering from HTOS will believe, with very little evidence, that a man she hardly knows is probably the one for her. She just "feels it." These women will say things like "I think he's my soul mate" after one date, or "I'm going to marry him" after one conversation. This is the most severe type of Oneitis, and can get you into a lot of trouble. Again, any of us can experience these sorts of thoughts or fantasies about a guy we hardly know, but HTOS girls don't recognize that it's fantasy.

The most important thing to realize is that no matter how strong a feeling you get for a guy you just met or dated once, that feeling doesn't necessarily mean he's the guy for you. It's certainly possible that he is, but it's more likely that he isn't. A more common scenario is that you meet a guy you like, date him, and then get the feeling after you get to know him—then he turns out to be the guy for you! Overall, don't put too much stock in strong feelings you get for a man you don't know well. Get to know him first.

Too Serious, Too Soon

Why do we date? To get to know someone and find out if they're a match for us, right? Well, this process takes time. A common mistake is to get too serious by wanting too much too soon. The following two examples illustrate what this looks like, and the trouble it can get you into.

William went on three dates with Katie, a woman he met through a friend. William travels a lot for work, sometimes for months at a time, and told Katie that he was leaving for a three-month assignment in Europe. They kept in touch while he was gone, and when he returned, he took her out to dinner. At that point, Katie wanted to get serious, and when William said he wasn't ready to, Katie got mad. She told him that she'd been waiting for him for three months, and how dare he waste her time.

Jeremy and Leann live in different states, and met at the airport. They kept in touch over e-mail, and then Leann invited Jeremy for a visit. After visiting each other's hometown once, Leann started planning how often they were going to see each other and wanted to draw up a schedule with Jeremy. She also mentioned that her company had a branch in his city and that it might be possible for her to transfer. Jeremy broke things off.

Both Katie and Leann got too serious too quickly. After only three dates, Katie put her dating life on hold for a guy who was in another country for three months. Leann started talking about moving to Jeremy's city after only a month. More importantly, in each case, the woman moved forward assuming that the guy was moving with her, when he wasn't.

Getting serious too soon, whether through your actions or through your words, is risky enough when both people want it, but it's a deal-killer when the guy isn't moving as fast as you, or isn't moving at all. Of all the dating mistakes women make with men, this one's a biggie—even nice guys who want a relationship get freaked out by this.

Here are some signs you may be moving too fast:

- You stop seeing or even considering other men within the first couple of dates
- You consider him a boyfriend and call him that with your friends or family, when you're still in the dating phase
- You expect exclusivity from him after only a few dates
- You want him to meet your family right away
- On the first couple of dates, you suggest doing an activity with him a month from now

Having done any of the above things doesn't mean there's something wrong with you. It just isn't an effective way to deal with men. Remember: things only work when both people feel the same way. Just because you're ready to move forward doesn't mean he is. Try to slow your pace to his, or if he's too pokey, move on to a different guy.

Premature Commitment

Premature commitment means focusing too much on one man, to the exclusion of others, before you really know him, how he feels, or if things are going somewhere. Most people think of commitment in terms of marriage, but in the dating world, commitment equals exclusivity. When you and he become exclusive, you date only each other. Exclusivity is a good thing, once you reach a certain point. But many women make this commitment before it is appropriate to do so. For example, Carla told me that she'd just ended a two-month relationship with Simon. Apparently, Simon was so busy with work that Carla saw him less than once per week. Sometimes he would booty-call her. Carla wondered if Simon was just not that interested in her, but was confused because he called her all the time. I quipped that if a guy I dated wasn't available, I would be out with a bunch of other guys in between dates with him. "Oh no," Carla said, "I was so into him from the start that I stopped seeing other men."

What was Carla's mistake? She fell for Simon and ruled out other men too quickly, before he proved he was worthy. If Simon had taken her out often, treated her well, and otherwise showed promise, then Carla's eventual lack of interest in other men would be understandable. But that wasn't the case.

Why Oneitis Is a Problem (Or Even a Turnoff)

As you learned earlier, Oneitis scares men off and generally gets in the way of your dating success. Here are some reasons for this.

Oneitis Looks Desperate

When you get serious too quickly or rule out other men right away, a guy may think that you just need to be with someone, or that you're insecure, needy, or desperate for marriage and kids. This will make him uncomfortable and will decrease your attractiveness. Even if you aren't desperate or needy, you will be perceived that way.

For example, Emily met a cute, funny guy through mutual friends. Zach seemed like a good guy so she agreed to go out with him. She had a nice time and at the end of the date, Zach told Emily he wasn't planning on seeing other women and wanted her to see only him. After one date! Emily liked Zach and had the feeling they would wind up in a relationship, yet she wasn't ready to be exclusive. But because Emily liked him, she said yes to his request. Sure enough, Zach turned out to be the most insecure man she'd ever dated and often did things to test her devotion to him. When Emily broke it off with Zach, he started dating someone else the very next day. The lesson here? Oneitis not only looks bad, it can actually be a bad sign.

Oneitis Makes Discrimination Difficult

If you recall from Mistake #4, being discriminating means knowing the type of guy and the type of relationship you want, and not dating people who don't fit that standard. But it's difficult to be discriminating when you're head-over-heels for a guy—you see only what you want to see! Even if he has what you're looking for up front, it takes time before you really know if he's the real deal. It's like buying a house without having it inspected—you may have a great feeling about the house (it's in a good neighborhood and has the extra bathroom and the hardwoods you wanted), but you don't know yet if it has foundation damage, termites, or a bad furnace.

Take Caitlin for example. She has been dating for a long time and is looking to meet the right guy. She's very clear on what she's looking for, and when she met Devin, she had a very good feeling about him right away. After a few dates, she saw that he had every quality on her list—she stopped seeing other men and fell head over heels for Devin. Soon, however, Devin started showing other sides of himself. One of her top requirements was that she wanted a man who was respectful; Devin was respectful at first, but then started making fun of her flaws and not calling when he said he would. She was so into Devin that she excused his behavior, until she realized he was wrong for her. Caitlin ended it after six weeks, and she was heartbroken.

Caitlin saw promise in Devin and developed a case of Oneitis. She didn't scare him off, but she forgot that it takes time to really get to know a man and faced a big disappointment as a result. You have to be discriminating not only when you first meet a man, but also while you date and get to know him.

Guys can pick up on a lack of discrimination. They can sense when a woman is too eager and when she needs a man rather than needing *him*. They know that commitment is serious and only to be bestowed upon the right person, and that it's impossible to know early on if your date is that person. You can suspect, you can hope, but you cannot know for sure, and you shouldn't behave as if you do. It takes many months or years to know if someone's right for you. So when you feel sold on a guy right away, he may assume you aren't discriminating.

Oneitis Is Overwhelming

While it's flattering when someone really likes you right away, it's a lot of pressure because you feel like you're responsible for their feelings. Think about a time when a guy came on too strong: maybe he called you too often. Maybe he complimented you too much. Maybe he wanted to move too fast, or pressured you to have sex. How did it make you feel? Did you feel overwhelmed or scared? When you expect a lot from a man too soon, that's how he'll feel.

In some cases, you and he will hit it off and both of you will want to move quickly. But this can backfire too. People, particularly men, can only handle so much intimacy at once—too much too soon can sabotage things.

Maybe you're not desperate, needy, indiscriminate, or any of the things guys fear. Maybe you just really liked a guy and got caught up in the excitement. And let's face it: some men do spook easily or get paranoid at any sign of possible entrapment. But even if men's fears are unfounded, why trigger them? As this book has shown you, a big part of success in dating is learning to see things from men's point of view. If Oneitis scares men, keep it under control.

If you're a hopeless romantic or tend to move fast, the important thing is to be aware of that and enjoy the feelings without letting them take over. In the next section, you'll learn how.

Turn Up the Volume

One reason you get fixated on a guy is because it feels like he's the only eligible, interesting guy within a 100-mile radius. But unless you live in the middle of nowhere, this isn't the case. Instead, you need to volumize. Volumizing is meeting, or at least being near, a lot of different men on a regular basis. It does *not* mean going out on countless dates with men who don't interest you that much. You don't have to date any of these men; you just have to be around them.

One challenge adults face today is that we aren't often exposed to that many people. We get into a routine and our worlds become small. We work in the same office, live in the same home, and hang out with the same friends. Unless you meet someone interesting in your office, neighborhood, or through your friends, you're out of luck. And when you do meet a fascinating guy, you might get Oneitis because he's the first interesting guy you've met in ages.

Volumizing expands your world, which accomplishes two things: One, it increases the number of people you interact with, which shows you that you have options. This is helpful when you meet someone you like and makes you much less prone to Oneitis. Why get all goo-goo over one guy when there are a bunch of other ones out there? Two, it increases the chances of meeting someone you like. Social scientists have looked at the factors that predict couples getting together—you know what the number one factor is? Proximity, or being near someone. Most couples meet because they work in the same office, belong to the same organizations, or went to the same high school. You can't meet new people if you do the same things day after day.

So how do you volumize? Probably not the way you think. When you tell a single person, male or female, to get out and meet new people, they often reply, "I'm not into the bar scene." If the bar scene is the first thing that comes to mind when you think of meeting new men, you definitely need to volumize! While it's possible to meet a good guy in a bar, it isn't that likely. Instead, do social things that you enjoy. Not only will you meet men who enjoy the same things you do, but you'll also feel more relaxed because you're doing something you like. I'm a runner, and I've met a ton of men in running groups. Other women I know meet men in hiking, mountaineering, cycling, or ski clubs. ports will always attract men, and the more competitive or challenging the sport, the more male-dominated it will be.

However, if sports aren't your thing, there are other options. Many cities have networking or social groups that meet during happy hour, attracting professional types who want to mix business with socializing. Many cities also have singles-oriented groups that host social activities. Museums and other cultural organizations have memberships that include parties, happy hours, and other social activities. There are also social clubs affiliated with religious groups, volunteering, sports events, bookstores, and coffee houses. Take a finance or investing class. And be sure to go to parties when you're invited.

You don't have to look at these activities as a way to pick up men. You don't have to date the men you meet. Just talk to them and be social. This way, you can "date" multitudes of men without ever having to go out on a date. And if you do start dating one, you'll have a better idea of what he's like than if you date a stranger. It's important to get out there and see how many men there are and to realize you're not the only single person in the world.

Play the Field

So I told you how much a pickup artist dreads a case of Oneitis. If he does catch it, how does he handle it? He plays the field by going out with a bunch of other women. This helps him get his mind off his Oneitis because he sees that there are lots of women out there. I'm not suggesting you should date men you aren't interested in to get your mind off your Oneitis; I'm saying that if you play the field, you're less likely to develop Oneitis in the first place.

These days, you'll find that a lot of people, male and female, don't like to play the field. Some feel that playing the field is wrong, that you should focus on one person at a time and not play games. Others feel it's just too complicated —they get overwhelmed by juggling different people or by having to face rejection (or rejecting) on a regular basis. Others feel it's impossible: "I can hardly get one date," they say. "How can I possibly play the field?" These are all legitimate concerns. But playing the field is perfectly legit, and can be very helpful for fighting off Oneitis as well as for finding the guy you want, for many reasons.

It's efficient. Dating multiple men allows you to check out numerous potential partners within a short amount of time. If you only date one person at a time, it could be years before you find the one you want to settle down with.

It takes the pressure off. When you date multiple men, you don't put so much pressure on any one guy, especially if there's one you like more than the others. This is a good way to handle Oneitis.

It shows that you're discriminating. Dating multiple men shows that you don't settle on the first guy who asks you out or who impresses you up front. It shows that you want to wait until a guy shows he's worth ruling out other guys for. It's easy to settle on the wrong guy when you don't have other options.

It shows that you have game. A man wants to feel like he has captured a great woman. He knows that sought-after women have other men to choose from, and if you wind up choosing him over them, he will really feel special.

It gives you a basis for comparison. When you date multiple men, it allows you to clearly see the differences between men, and which ones have what you want. This is a lot easier than comparing your date with men from your past.

It means less disappointment. When it doesn't work out with one of your dates, either because you realize he isn't for you, or because he stops calling, you know you have others to spend time with. There are always other men.

Part of what people, especially women, find distasteful about playing the field is that they assume playing the field means being a player. But a player doesn't want a relationship and wants to enjoy the freedom of seeing as many people as possible. Players, who are typically men, have a bad reputation because many of them are only interested in sexual conquests and will deceive, play games, or lie in order to achieve that goal. These men may treat a woman like a girlfriend, even calling her a girlfriend, while getting some on the side with other women. When you come across these kinds of men, it's no wonder that you associate playing the field with playing. However, they aren't the same thing.

Playing the field is dating multiple people until you find one you want to be exclusive with. Most of the time, you can tell within a few dates whether a man has potential for a relationship or not. If he doesn't, you move on. Once you find a man who you like and who wants commitment, you stop seeing the others. You do not lie or trick anyone.

Here's an example of how playing the field works, and why it can be beneficial:

Tori started dating online and met two guys she liked. She was more interested in Darren than she was in Jordan, and things went really well on her first few dates with Darren. But she didn't feel she knew Darren well yet, and kept seeing Jordan. On the next date with Darren, Tori noticed that he was moody and made rude comments about his ex. She backed away from Darren, and Jordan started to look more interesting. Soon, she dumped Darren and kept seeing Jordan.

If Tori had stopped seeing Jordan and focused on Darren because she felt strongly about him, she probably would have developed Oneitis, gotten too involved with Darren, and eventually gotten hurt. This is why playing the field is powerful; it keeps things in check.

If you choose to play the field, here are some ground rules:

Be honest. When you first start dating a guy, there's no reason to tell him you're seeing others. You'll weed out most guys before it even becomes an issue. It's more of an issue when you're still seeing a guy after multiple dates, especially if you sense genuine interest in him. At that point, he'll probably be looking to move forward, so it's a good time to be honest. If you still want to see him, say so, but say you aren't ready to stop seeing others yet.

Be careful about sex. Because sex is a touchy issue, the best way to avoid problems is to avoid sex with men until you are exclusive. Men are weird about sex. Many don't sleep around, but most, including the ones who do, don't like when a woman sleeps with someone other than him. You may not like the double standard, but it's there, like it or not. Sexual involvement with more than one man gets complicated. Plus, there's the issue of safe sex. Ultimately, your sex life is your business, and you don't owe any man your sexual exclusivity if you don't want to give it. Just be sure to use condoms, and be clear that you are not exclusive with him.

Don't talk about other dates. Don't discuss other men you're seeing. If he asks you about it, don't feel you have to explain anything to him. It's none of his business. As long as he knows you're still dating others, you've done your part.

Don't mind men who don't want to play. Some men may not want to share you with other men. Don't give in to this pressure if you aren't ready to stop seeing other men. Just like you can't make a man only see you, he can't make you only see him. He can deal with it, or choose to move on.

Be respectful. Seeing other men means having lots of options. But you should still treat the men you date with respect. Don't be a flake: if you make a date, keep it. If you don't want to see one of your guys anymore, let him know respectfully that you aren't interested.

Don't see him too often. If you see a man multiple times a week, but still want to see other men, it will confuse him because it sends mixed messages. If you're dating multiple men, try to see each of them only once per week or so.

Take It Slow

If you want to avoid Oneitis and the damage it can do, learn to slow things down. As you've learned, moving too quickly is a sure way to scare a guy off. It's also a sure way to become entwined with a guy who turns out to be a jerk. To avoid this mistake, here are some guidelines to follow:

Remind yourself that you don't know him yet. No matter how attracted you are to a guy, or how great he may seem, you don't know him yet. He could still turn out to be a toad, and you don't want to get too involved before you find this out. Getting to know a guy takes a long time.

Avoid sex. Sexual intimacy can develop more quickly than emotional intimacy; in other words, people often have sex before they know how they feel about each other. Then, emotional intimacy is forced to catch up—there will be pressure to move forward, and some people (especially men) may not feel ready to. Unfortunately, in most cases, you will have to be the one to put on the brakes when it comes to sex. This isn't easy, but it's easier when you do two things: decide ahead of the date that you aren't going to have sex, and don't go to each other's homes.

Avoid getting too personal. If sexual intimacy can rush things, so can emotional intimacy. Get to know each other a little at a time. Stick with discussing work, hobbies, and friends, and keep the life goals, childhood issues, and ex files at bay for a while. And be careful about discussing marriage and children. If you're too eager, he may think, *She wants marriage and kids, and I'm the latest interviewee for the job of sperm donor and provider.* There's nothing wrong with being ready for marriage and kids, just be careful how and when you say it.

Avoid seeing him too often. When you're early in the dating process with a man, don't see him too often. Restrict your dating to one date per week, two maximum. This sends the message that you are not desperate, and it gives a man time to process how he feels about you. Many people, especially men, need space to develop feelings for someone. If he asks to see you more than that, simply tell him you have other plans. For the same reason, also avoid talking on the phone too often.

Let him set the pace. Men often move a little slower than women at the start of a relationship. So let him dictate when you guys go out and when things get more serious. Don't try and nail him down for future activities—you may not be dating him in the future! Planning for a concert in a month is something couples do, not people who just started dating. If he hasn't mentioned the L word or meeting the family, don't bring it up. If you give it time, and if he's genuinely interested in you, he will bring up meeting family and future events when he's ready. Waiting until he's ready shows respect for his needs, and shows that you're independent.

Know When to Commit

So you've been volumizing and playing the field, and you meet Mr. Special. When should you make a commitment to exclusivity and stop seeing other guys? Here are some guidelines:

You've been dating a while. By a "while," I mean you've had multiple successful dates. You've had a chance to get to know one another and have a consistent history of phone calls and dates. Both Carla and Katie violated this guideline: Carla stopped seeing other men before she and Simon showed a consistent string of dates, and Katie wanted exclusivity from William after only three dates and a three-month absence.

He's giving you what you need (so far). At this early stage, getting what you need means that he calls you often, you see him regularly, you enjoy his company, he treats you well, and he seems interested in you. Things are going well, and you have a good feeling about it. Clearly, Simon wasn't fulfilling Carla's needs—she broke up with him because he rarely made himself available to her. It made little sense for her to stop seeing other men. She should have waited to see if Simon gave her what she needed, then considered exclusivity. Katie didn't get her needs met either—William was in another country for three months and didn't try to visit her or have her visit him. Don't put the cart before the horse—give exclusivity if, and only if, your needs are already being met.

You've discussed and agreed upon exclusivity. Most couples, after getting to know one another, will discuss this issue one way or another. One woman's guy asked her if she were seeing someone else; when she said no, he said he wasn't either, and that he was glad. Another woman's guy was more formal, and said sweetly, "Would you be my girlfriend?" However you do it, make sure you have this conversation. If he wants exclusivity, he'll hint or outright ask questions to see if you're seeing anyone else or to let you know he isn't. Never assume exclusivity. This is true even if you're having sex and seeing each other all the time. If you want to know, ask.

Dating is a way to have fun, but ultimately, it's a way to see if these men are relationship material. The process of determining whether a man is relationship material takes time, and determining if he's marriage material takes even longer. Yet many women forget this fact, to their own detriment.

Don't beat yourself up if you've let Oneitis take hold of you. It can happen to anyone. The trick is to be aware of it and not let it make bad decisions for you. And once you've caught Oneitis and then learned that Mr. Right was really Mr. Totally Wrong, you're less likely to let it happen again!

Mistake #10

You Listen to Your Mother

"When your mother asks, 'Do you want a piece of advice?' it is a mere formality. It doesn't matter if you answer yes or no. You're going to get it anyway."

ERMA BOMBECK

Recently, a friend of mine ended a long-term relationship. She's very outgoing, so once she started dating again, she would share her dating stories with everyone she knows in order to get their advice. But after several weeks of this, she'd had enough, and said to me, "My God, everyone is an expert! You will not believe the bad advice I've gotten from people!"

Actually, I would. When it comes to dating, people have strong opinions. And why not? Everyone can relate to the challenges of dating. Your family, friends, boss, and even the woman who cuts your hair will have plenty of advice for you. And thanks to the miracle of the web, you can get advice through various forums and chat sites, and anyone can start a website or blog to dispense their advice. The good thing about all these sources of advice is that you can usually find help when you need it. The bad news? The help isn't always helpful.

Take Brandy for example. Brandy was unhappy because she had a pattern of getting into relationships with men who treated her poorly. She wrote to an online advice columnist, who was a self-titled male "expert," for advice on how to deal with this problem. This guy's answer? That Brandy stayed with these men because, deep down, she liked being treated that way. If she didn't like being treated that way, he reasoned, she wouldn't date those men.

How much do you think this genius's advice helped this woman? I'd say somewhere between very little and not at all. It probably made her feel worse!

So while there's a lot of bad advice out there, there's also a lot of advice that may be totally fine, but not that helpful for your particular situation or personality style. Also, you've probably found that, at times, the advice you receive from one person totally conflicts with advice from someone else. For example, you went out on a date with a guy and you haven't heard from him in four days. When you tell your friends about it, one friend tells you he's just busy, another one tells you he's not interested, and still another friend tells you to just call him. Meanwhile, you're thinking, *What the hell do I do?*

If you want to survive dating, you must find yourself a good support system. No matter how smart or experienced you are, you need people to talk to and to advise you. Dating is a time when we look for the man we may wind up spending the rest of our lives with—good support is crucial. Unfortunately, the right kind of support can be hard to find! Just because people have strong opinions or have been in your situation doesn't mean their advice is any good! And, frankly, bad advice is worse than no advice. Women are good about asking others' advice, but we don't always seek the kind of support we need most. Because a good support system is so important in dating, this section will talk about what that is and how to find it.

Not-So-Good Advice

There are many difference types of advice. But regardless of the nature of the advice and who's giving it, advice should have two qualities: it should be helpful and it should be supportive. Likewise, not-so-good advice is either unhelpful, unsupportive, or both.

Unhelpful Advice

The purpose of asking for advice is to get help with a problem you're having. Ideally, you get some answers that make sense and help you solve the problem. Not all advice you receive will be helpful to you; if you're dating a guy who has alcohol abuse problems, not everyone will know how to help you. But there are some types of advice that are particularly unhelpful, such as when your advice-giver is totally inexperienced. For example, you like a guy you've gone out with a few times, but now he's calling you multiple times per day. When you ask your friend her opinion, she tells you he really likes you and you should feel flattered! This advice isn't that helpful to you because it lacks insight; a guy who calls that often, that soon in a relationship, is coming on way too strong.

As another example, what about the genius above, who told Brandy that she dates men who treat her badly because she enjoys being treated badly? Clearly, not helpful! If this advice-giver had any insight, he would know that nobody *likes* being treated badly, and if Brandy really did like it she wouldn't have written him for advice! His advice lacked any deeper understanding of women, dating, and human behavior. Yet another example of unhelpful advice is when a guy tells you to chase men and come on strong; he advises you to do this because not because it's the best course of action for you, but because it's what he would want. He's had bad luck with women and doesn't want to take any risks. This is bad advice because while it never hurts to show a guy you're interested, you shouldn't chase him. His advice is about his needs, not yours.

Unsupportive Advice

The other reason we seek advice is to have someone listen to us, understand where we're coming from, and show us that they're on our side. When we seek advice, more often than not we're looking for support more than actual advice. Unhelpful advice is no fun because you can't get the help you need. Unsupportive advice, however, really sucks—it makes you feel foolish, ashamed, or hopeless, and winds up making you feel worse rather than better. Unsupportive advice-givers all have one thing in common: they have their own issues and they're projecting them onto you. They may call their advice "tough love," but most of the time it isn't love at all. Unfortunately, there are several types of unsupportive advisers:

The Critic. The Critic analyzes your dating behavior and finds things wrong with your approach, and, of course, tells you what they are. The Critic will say things like "You'd be really attractive if you lost weight" or "You're going to end up single if you keep doing that." While some honest advice about your weaknesses can be very helpful, Critics aren't nice about it and seem to enjoy finding flaws in your approach to dating.

The Devil's Advocate. If you're having a problem with a guy, the DA takes the guy's side or focuses on his perspective. If you complain to a DA that a guy you're dating made a rude comment to you, she'll defend him and say he was having a bad day and to give him a break. Sometimes, it can be extremely helpful to look at both sides of every issue and try to see things from a man's point of view. But the purpose of seeking support from others is to focus more on you and your perspective, and the DA doesn't do that.

The Blamer. Blamers love to tell you that your dating problems are your fault. "It's your own fault he didn't call. You slept with him on the first date!" she'll say. There is a difference between taking responsibility and taking blame; if you're having dating problems, it's important that you look hard at what you're doing to contribute to them. However, having someone blame you for your dating troubles doesn't help and only makes you feel worse. The right advice in this situation would be, "That really sucks. I'm sorry he hasn't called. Do you think it might be better to wait longer to have sex next time?"

The Naysayer. Whatever you want to do, the Naysayer will poo-poo it. If you want to date multiple men, she'll tell you it's too hard or that men won't put up with it. If you want to get married, she'll tell you that marriage sucks. If you want to date younger men, she'll tell you younger men are immature or don't like older women. I've had people naysay me many times—I just smile and ignore them because they're always wrong. Just because it didn't work for them doesn't mean it won't work for me! Don't let anyone tell you that you can't have what you want.

There is one more type of not-so-good advice: unsolicited advice! These people will tell you what to do when you never even asked! But if you talk about your problems to people, they'll assume you're looking for help. A good rule of thumb: don't talk about any dating challenge with anyone you don't want advice from.

The Top Three Sources of (Not-So-Helpful) Advice

When they have dating problems, most women seek advice and support from three main sources: mothers, friends, and dating experts. All three can be excellent sources of advice. But, just because they're the most natural places to turn to for advice doesn't mean all mothers, girlfriends, and dating experts are good advice-givers. This section covers the pros and cons of each.

Mothers

Because your mom is older and more experienced than you and is the woman you've known the longest, it's natural to turn to your mom for advice. Ideally, a mom is helpful because she's experienced, and she's supportive because she's, well, your mom! She loves you and wants you to be happy. But mothers aren't always the best source of advice.

While moms are older and more experienced, they come from a different generation and may have outdated advice. For example, how many of you have mothers who've advised you to marry a man with money, marry a doctor, or marry a guy you aren't attracted to because he'd be a good provider? To some extent, marrying money made sense in the past when women didn't have a lot of power in society and relied on a man to support her and her children. Today, while a guy with money is nice, a woman can earn her own. And marrying a guy you're not that attracted to won't work: in this day and age, women want a romantic partner, not just a provider!

Other moms may be more modern or savvy, but their advice is still based on their own experiences. If your mom married at twenty, her dating experience will be limited, and so will her ability to advise you. And your mom has probably never dated online, speed-dated, or even used condoms! Overall, advice that's outdated or based on limited experience isn't that helpful.

And, unfortunately, Mom's advice isn't always supportive either. Moms can be critical, blaming, and all the other forms of unsupportive. Mothers are often more critical of their daughters than they are of anyone else—they project their insecurities and fears onto their daughters and criticize when, deep down, they want to help. How many of you get grief from your mom because you aren't married yet? How many of you have been criticized for dating a certain guy Mom didn't like, or for breaking up with a guy she did like?

Overall, be very careful with Mom's advice. If you find that she consistently gives you unhelpful or unsupportive advice, stop asking her opinion and seek counsel elsewhere. If she's the difficult type that will still give advice, simply say you don't want to talk about it and ask her advice about other things. You may have to repeat yourself a few times, but be very firm about it. Of course, if you do find your mom's advice helpful or supportive, get all you can. Even if she's helpful in some areas but not others, tap her knowledge in those areas and toss the rest.

Girlfriends

Girlfriends are often a more satisfying source of advice than moms. You have more in common with your girlfriends, they understand you better, they're your age, and they don't usually have that motherly tendency to be critical. But girlfriends can dole out bad advice too.

One of the more common problems with girlfriends is that they often don't know any more than you do. They're still dating and learning just like you are. And the married ones can't always relate to your situation because they're too busy raising kids and trying to make a marriage work! Also, depending on where they are in their personal lives, girlfriends can give bad advice. For example, when Nora felt like she was falling too hard for a guy who seemed distant, her friend Karen told her to sleep with another guy to keep herself emotionally more distant!

Girlfriends may not always know everything, but one of the best things about them is that they're supportive. They listen, they hear your point of view, they let you vent, they analyze with you, and they stick by you when you're struggling and when you've been hurt. That's what they're for! Unfortunately, some girlfriends take on a more "mother-like" role and can be critical or nagging rather than supportive. The reason some friends do this is similar to why moms do it—their own personal issues get in the way of their ability to help you.

When you're dating, keep as many girlfriends around as you can for advice. But remember that they may not know all the answers. And if you find that they're not supportive in their advice, avoid talking to them about dating.

Dating Experts

Because our moms and friends don't know everything, sometimes we turn to experts. We read advice columns on the web, buy dating books, and even go to a therapist from time to time. Experts can be a good addition to your mom or girlfriends because they usually have more knowledge, training, and insight. However, experts have their flaws too.

On the web, you'll find that advice ranges from decent to horrible. There are many reputable sites, but a lot of what's out there is garbage. Reputable advice-givers give helpful and supportive advice; if the advice seems silly or game-like, or if the source is critical or makes insulting comments about women or men, avoid it. Fortunately for you, a lot of the bad web advice out there is actually aimed at *men*—some of these sites ask men to pay for advice, promising them that if they follow it they can get any woman they want or have beautiful women swarming around them.

Even with reputable experts and therapists, each has his or her own bias or view of the world. Their advice will reflect this worldview and may be good advice for some people, but not for others. For example, some experts feel strongly that women ask for too much in their search for a man and encourage women to lower their standards. While it's always good to have realistic standards, these experts ask women to compromise on crucial items like chemistry or values. These experts value getting married over having a highly compatible partner, so the advice isn't good for women who want more than to just get a man to marry her.

Another example is experts who advise you to play games when you date. Some will tell you to never, ever call a man. Others will tell you to wait for an engagement ring before you sleep with a man. And still others will tell you that it's perfectly fine to use men for free dinners. These experts have very old-fashioned ideas about men and women; they perceive men as having more power in the dating world, and games are a way to take power back. While we have to deal with men a little differently than we deal with women, by now you should know that women have a lot of power in the dating world. You should never have to play games; they only make you look weak.

And unfortunately, some experts can be shockingly unsupportive. I've seen experts tell their advisees to "stop whining." Experts like Dr. Laura Schlessinger often criticize and browbeat women for their mistakes. Some popular dating books shame women, as if every dating failure is their fault: If your man cheated, it's because *you* did something wrong; if he treats you bad, it's because *you* just weren't interesting enough to him or because *you* didn't follow some rule of dating. While it's always necessary to take responsibility for your role in your dating problems, you aren't responsible for a man's bad behavior. Despite this fact, these "experts" feel the need to blame women. How on earth is this helpful? If you read the bestselling *How to Win Friends and Influence People*, Dale Carnegie will tell you that criticizing and shaming people is the last way to get them to change!

I must mention one more source of potentially bad advice: guys. I don't include it above because most women don't seek out guys for advice. There's good reason for this: when it comes to dating and relationships, a lot of guys aren't that helpful or supportive! Often, their advice is based on what they'd want, rather than what's best for you. Many men tend to oversimplify: for example, you tell a guy you're nervous about a date and he says, "Don't be nervous." Or, if you dated a jerk, he'll tell you to stop dating jerks and date nice guys. And they're not always the best about making you feel better.

There are exceptions: some men are insightful about women and relationships and can give good advice. I've known many men like this and ask their opinions often. Some men can be very supportive, too. If you find a guy like this, keep him in your rotation of advisers.

There's an interesting difference between dating advice for women and dating advice for men: men are encouraged to go for what they want, whereas women more often are expected to settle. In society, it's not that surprising when a man wants to be a millionaire or King of the World. But when a woman wants to, people think she's aiming out of her league! It's the same in dating: if a man wants to date a woman half his age, people might make fun of him, but they accept it. If a woman wants to date some hottie half her age, they think she's a freak! This double standard is everywhere, so beware. Don't let anyone tell you that you can't have what you want!

Remember: any and all advice reflects the person giving it. The advice is about where that person is coming from, and the more limited that person's perspective, and the more different that person is from you, the less helpful the advice will be. Even if the advice itself is sound, it may not be what's best for you given your situation.

So What Is Good Advice?

Although you've already learned that good advice is both helpful and supportive, I want to elaborate on what that means. The following is a discussion of a few hallmarks of good dating advice. Overall, good advice should be:

Sympathetic. When you tell people your dating challenges and ask for advice, you want advisers who sympathize with your situation, even if they can't relate to it directly. They should stand by you, even when you make mistakes.

Honest. While kindness and support are important, you still want someone who can be honest with you. If you're coming on too strong to men, you want someone who can say so and help you come up with a better strategy.

Tailored to your needs. Dating advice should reflect what you need more than what your adviser would need. For example, your friend may not mind if her boyfriend smokes pot, but if she knows you hate the stuff, she shouldn't give you a hard time because you're thinking of dumping a guy who smokes it.

Respectful of your limits. An adviser should understand that you aren't perfect and may make mistakes. A friend of mine who is striking, smart, and kind, was dating a guy who was, to put it bluntly, a total asshole. He flirted with other women constantly, criticized her, and didn't work half the time. When she split up with him, I was ecstatic. But she was miserable without him. Eventually, they got back together, and I was horrified and could not believe she'd go back. But despite this, I didn't hassle her and supported her as best I could. I knew she was doing the best she could and what felt right to her at the time. Eventually, she dumped him for good, met a great guy who treated her well, and married him. Every woman has to learn her own lessons, her own way.

The Best Source of Advice

Even the best advisers may not give you what you need. If you're anything like me, you've had times in your life where you've encountered a particular dating problem and not one person you talked to had a solution for you. After this happened to me, say, 100 times, I finally started looking to a different source to answer my questions: myself! You will find, many times, that you are your best source of advice!

Are you serious? you're probably asking. *If I had the answers to my own dating problems, I wouldn't need advice ever!* It's true that you don't have all the answers. Nobody does. But you'll find that you are the best roadmap to finding them. Much of the time, no mother, friend, or expert can give you answers to your problems—all they can do is help you find your own answers.

Dealing with dating difficulties, like dealing with other personal issues, isn't the same as dealing with your credit card debt or leaky roof. These latter problems have clear solutions: we can hire a financial adviser to help us get the debt under control and a handyman to fix the roof. But with dating, there is no expert that completely knows what's best for you; they can't look into your brain, heart, or soul and find something to fix or know exactly what you need. Only you can do that.

So how do you do this? You do it by learning to listen to your instincts. Some people call it listening to your heart, your soul, your gut, your intuition, or your inner knowing —whatever you choose to call it, it is an amazing source of wisdom. It knows what's best for you and what you need, better than anyone else. And it should be what guides you when you date and look for the right man. It's perfectly fine, and even helpful, to seek out advice from others; but ultimately you should follow your own instincts to make dating decisions.

To illustrate this point, I'll give you an example from my life. I once dated a guy who had the qualities I look for in a man. I really liked him, and he liked me. Even though he lived far away from me, I was willing to accept that and see how things went. Even though he visited, called regularly, and seemed interested in me, I often didn't feel good about the relationship. I didn't feel secure, like something was missing. And he'd said some things about his ex that I didn't like. A friend told me I should just relax, that things were going well and that long-distance relationships take time. Another friend told me she could tell my guy was interested in me, and to not make a big deal about the things he said. So, I stuck it out.

But things did not get better. Finally, he did something I didn't like and we got into a big argument. I got angry, he got defensive, and we found ourselves at a stalemate. Suddenly, the answers came to me: he seemed like my type of guy, but he was totally wrong for me. I was so busy trying to make it work that I didn't realize I wasn't happy. So, I walked away from the relationship. Afterward, I realized he wasn't as available as I needed. He lived far away, for one thing—I wanted someone I could spend time with on a regular basis. And he was somewhat emotionally unavailable, which is why his comments about his ex didn't sit well with me. Ultimately, no one could give me those answers. I had to find them myself.

Your friends can offer their opinion on a guy or advise you on what to wear on a date, but some things are more complicated and require you to listen more carefully to your instincts.

Here are some areas where instincts can steer you in the right direction:

- Which men interest you (and which men don't)
- Which men to date (and which men to turn down)
- When to sleep with a man (and when to avoid sex)
- When to stop seeing a man (and when to give him another chance)

- Which men to get serious with (and when to get serious)

The best advice, regardless of where it comes from, is the advice that's best for you and what you need at the time. Fortunately, we have an endless supply of that advice—from ourselves. The hard part is learning to listen to it.

Dating on Instinct

Now that you know that your instincts can guide you in your dating life, here are a few different techniques you can use to date successfully.

Ditch the Games

Have you ever noticed that dating advice is often . . . well, gamey? People are so baffled by dating that they come up with these ridiculous ploys to help them deal with the challenges. By contrast, if you ever read a book on how to succeed at marriage, it will have plenty of advice and rules to follow, but none of them are stupid or gamey. Well, games have no place in dating either.

Here are some common examples of game-like dating advice:

Games women are told to play	Games men are told to play
Wait two days to call him back	Wait five days to call her
Be mysterious	Act like you don't care
Don't tell him you love him	Rarely tell her you love her
Don't be too good to him	Don't be too nice to her

See any pattern here? Both sexes are basically told the same dumb things, hoping that it will help them succeed at dating. Games are for people who don't know how to deal with the opposite sex. But once you start listening to your instincts, you'll get better at knowing if a guy's interested, if you should call or wait, or if you should express your feelings or hold back. You won't need to play games.

Make Your Own Rules

If dating advice can be gamey, it can also be filled with rules, most of which are followed by ominous warnings of what will happen to you if you break them. Basically, if you don't obey some commonly believed dating rule, you'll never attract the right guy and will be doomed to become a nun who spends her life gardening and teaching orphans to read! Or something like that. Another problem with rules is that the rulebooks have different rules. You try one, it fails, so you try the other and it fails too! Now what?

It's a mistake to follow other people's dating rules. Part of being successful at dating is figuring out what works for you—i.e., figuring out your own rules. Here are situations where it's helpful to make your own rules:

Whether to call a guy or ask him out. On the one hand, men are generally the pursuers and do the calling and asking out. On the other, women shouldn't have to sit by passively waiting, and guys like when women take up some of the slack. So what do you do? Follow any guidelines that make sense to you and choose what feels right for that situation, based on how shy or bold he is or how interested he seems. For example, if you sense that a guy wants to ask you out but is too shy, suggest getting together sometime. Or, if you want to call a guy but sense that it's too soon, wait a day or two. If something doesn't work or turn out how you wanted it to, make adjustments for next time.

When to have sex. This subject has created considerable debate among women, and is an area where women tend to judge each other, and themselves. Sex is important, and personal. It has consequences, emotional and otherwise. You'll hear rules from one end of the spectrum to the other, from sleeping with him right away to know what you're getting into, to the "third-date rule," to waiting a certain arbitrary number of months, or waiting until you're exclusive, until he proposes, or until you get married. But there's really only one right time to start having sex with a man: when it's the right time for you. For most women, that won't be on the first date—she's either not ready or she doesn't trust him enough yet. We all know a successful couple who's been together for years and who slept together on their first date. But there are many other women for whom that did not work.

Many women feel that sex is something precious and sacred that you "give up" when you have sex with a man. Others feel it's something fun and exciting that they want to share. Every woman is different. Never let anyone tell you to go against your personal instincts and feelings when it comes to sex. Do what you feel is right; if it doesn't work, you can change it.

Listen to Your Own Comfort Level
Instead of relying on games, rules, or even others' advice to tell you what to do in a dating situation, learn to rely

more on your feelings. Instead of making the mistake I made with the long-distance guy, pay more attention to how things feel instead of how they should feel. If something doesn't feel right, there is often a good reason, even if you (and your advisers) don't know what it is yet. Here is a good example of this:

Elisa met Kyle not long after she'd ended a three-year relationship. After seeing Kyle for about a month, things were starting to get more serious. At that time, Kyle told Elisa he'd also been seeing another woman during that month, and that he liked them both. Elisa appreciated Kyle's honesty, but felt weird about the situation. Kyle asked her to stick around; she said she'd get back to him. Elisa consulted her friend Olga. Olga told Elisa she was overreacting, that Kyle had every right to see other people, and that it was silly for Elisa to want an exclusive relationship after only being single for such a short time. Olga's argument made sense, so she continued to see Kyle. A few weeks later, Kyle told Elisa he wanted to pursue a relationship with the other girl. Elisa felt sad briefly, but mostly felt relieved. They stayed friends and had lunch from time to time. Elisa and her ex ended up getting back together, and they were very happy. A month or two later, Kyle hit on Elisa, and then told her he often thought about her when he was with his girlfriend. Elisa told Kyle she'd gotten back with her ex and made it clear she wasn't interested, and Kyle reacted with jealousy. Elisa stopped hanging out with Kyle, ignored his calls, and never saw him again.

Elisa's story is a good example of listening to others' advice instead of trusting her instincts. Elisa stopped feeling comfortable with Kyle once she found out he was seeing another woman. She didn't feel Kyle's behavior was wrong, like Olga assumed—the situation just didn't feel right to her. Yet she stayed because she didn't yet trust her own instincts. Sure enough, Kyle turned out to be a jerk who cared more about himself than either of the two women. Elisa told me that she still gets the "icks" whenever she thinks about Kyle. "If only I'd listened to my instincts, I could have saved myself that feeling," she said.

This is also a good example of not-so-good advice from a friend. Olga was not only unsupportive, but her advice didn't factor in Elisa's needs. Olga gave advice that would have worked for her rather than what was best for Elisa.

When we're dating or facing some sort of dating quandary, sometimes it's easy to focus on rules or follow others' advice because we don't always know what to do. But, if you pay close attention, you'll often detect a subtle discomfort or bad feeling—that's your gut's way of telling you to back off or try a different tactic.

Get a Good Support System

Even though I'm encouraging you to hone in on your instincts to make dating decisions, you should still get a good support system of friends, experts, and anyone else who can help. Why? No matter how good you become at trusting yourself, you still need someone to talk to for encouragement and support, especially if you've been rejected or disappointed. Talking it out helps you get through it so you can move on.

Also, even though your supporters' advice may not be what you need, it can help you cut through the confusion and get to those answers hidden deep inside of you. Listen to what people have to say; then, make your own decision. Personally, I only take about 2 percent of the advice I get from others; but I do use their advice to help me figure out my own solution.

Finally, to get good support, be a good support system for your single friends. When you advise, try to help your friend dig down and find her own inner wisdom. Often, you'll see that she knows what feels right to her, but needs your stamp of approval.

Your instincts are incredibly useful when it comes to dating. They can steer you away from the wrong men, draw you toward good ones, and generally guide you to situations that may be what you need at that time. This does not mean that you will not struggle—but if you listen to your own wisdom, the struggle will often lead to something good.

Every time I've been confused about dating, gotten advice, and put that advice before what my instincts were telling me, I've regretted it. The tricky thing about listening to our instincts is that they work much more quickly than our brains do. We may have a bad feeling about something and have no idea why. In Elisa and Kyle's case, Elisa wasn't comfortable with Kyle's seeing another woman, but her brain didn't understand why. That's why she consulted Olga. Eventually, Elisa figured out that Kyle wasn't a good guy and that the situation didn't have what she needed.

Learning to hone in on your deeper instincts takes practice. But, with time and effort, you'll learn to listen to yourself more and question yourself less. This will considerably improve your dating life, and other areas of your life too.

Conclusion

As you were reading this book, maybe you wondered if I've made any of the Top 10 Mistakes. The answer is . . . uh, yeah! I've made some more than others, but I've made them. The truth is, it's impossible to avoid mistakes in dating, just like in any area of life. The important thing is that we learn from the mistakes and keep going.

You're probably also wondering if I take my own advice. The answer is . . . absolutely. I have my weak moments, but I do follow my own guidelines because I believe in them. And I can tell you that not only did following them make dating more worthwhile, they helped me find my guy. My goal is that this book will help you do the same! Happy dating!

About the Author

Dr. Christie Hartman is a psychologist, researcher, and author who has conducted extensive research on dating and relationships. She is the author of *Dating the Divorced Man: Sort through the Baggage to Decide if He's Right for You* (*www.datingthedivorcedman.com*). This book provides detailed information and advice on all aspects of dating divorced men, and as one reader put it, "This book is a MUST READ for anyone considering dating a man who is either separated, divorcing, divorced, or still married but shopping for a girlfriend."

Dr. Hartman has appeared on national television, including *Fox News Live* and the *Weekend Today Show*, and has made numerous radio appearances across the United States. She did a book signing at the Tattered Cover Bookstore in Denver, which has hosted countless bestselling authors, from Barack Obama to Naomi Wolf. She's been interviewed by journalists and quoted in articles published on national sites such as CNN.com and Match.com.

Dr. Hartman works for the University of Colorado, where she's a researcher who studies adolescent drug abuse and conduct problems. She resides in Denver and enjoys the outdoors: she's a runner who has completed two marathons and several half-marathons, she's hiked eight 14ers (mountains over 14,000 feet), and she enjoys skiing. Dr. Hartman can be contacted through her website: *www.christie hartman.com*.

Index

Advantage. *See also* Power
  coming on too strong and,
    105–6
  games women play to gain,
    13–16
  getting, over men, 4–5
  men knowing women have,
    9–11
  real power and, 17–18
  tricks men play to gain, 10–11
  why men don't have, 5–9
  why women think men have,
    11–13
Advice
  about: overview of, 213–14
  best source of, 224–27
  from dating experts, 220–23
  from girlfriends, 219–20
  good, 214–15, 223–24
  from mothers, 218–19
  on playing games, 227–28
  support system and, 40–41,
    231–32
  top sources of not-so-helpful,
    218–23
  unhelpful, 215–16
  unsupportive, 216–18
  written for men, reading,
    108–10
Age
  concerns about, 30–31, 98–99,
    124–27
  lying about, 104–5
  men and younger women,
    98–99

  older women/younger men,
    125–27, 152, 177–78
  relationship readiness and,
    177–78
Attitudes (bad)
  #1: Not respecting men, 24–27,
    36
  #2: Believing Scarcity Myth,
    27–31, 36
  #3: Nursing old wounds,
    31–32, 36–37
  #4: Complaining to friends,
    32–33, 37
  #5: Making no effort, 33–35, 37
  affecting experience, 23–24
  bitterness and, 127
  blame and, 38, 39, 54, 217, 222
  common thread linking, 35
  difficulty of dating and, 39
  first step to cure, 35–38
  letting go of past and, 36–37,
    41–42
  negativity and, 106
  strategies to improve, 39–42
  taking responsibility and, 35–38,
    39
Attraction
  ease of, men vs. women, 9
  how men approach dating and,
    100–102
  sexual vs. emotional feelings
    and, 102
  stereotypes/truths of men and,
    98–100